# Double Image

## Biblical Insights from African Parables

by
*Del Tarr*

ILLUSTRATED BY JOHN L. WEIDMAN

Paulist Press
New York and Mahwah, N.J.

Library of Congress Cataloging-in-Publication Data

Tarr, Delbert Howard.
    Double image: biblical insights from African parables / by Del Tarr;
illustrated by John L. Weidman.
        p.   cm.
    Includes bibliographical references and index.
    ISBN 0-8091-3469-1
    1. Bible–Criticism, Narrrative. 2. Christianity and culture. 3. Africa,
West–Civilization–Philosophy. 4. Folk literature–Africa, West. 5. Jesus
Christ–Parables. 6. Storytelling–Religious aspects–Christianity. I. Title.
BS521.7.T37    1994
220.6'1–dc20                                                        94-2645
                                                                        CIP

Published by Paulist Press
997 Macarthur Boulevard
Mahwah, New Jersey 07430

Printed and bound in the
United States of America

# Table of Contents

iii

## TO 6
### TARR BABIES

Dolly, who accepted this black sticky name 40 years ago. This beautiful lady has followed me all over the world—and set up house 32 times.

Cindy Sharon and
Terry Mark and
Randel Ray...our own children.

Ainslie Katrice and
Luke Anton...our grandbabies.

Plus Jon, Wendi, and Becky. They married into this tribe and bring wonderful diversity to its shape.

# List of Illustrations

# Introduction

An African hunter, whether or not he has ever owned a gun, has learned to depend on the heightened ability of his natural senses to find and outwit skittish African game. I have seen western hunters, loaded to the teeth with high-powered paraphernalia, go crashing through the bush, either on foot or in a Land Rover, scaring the game hundreds of yards ahead and seldom getting sight of anything!

Perceiving game (sight and sound and smell) is an art to be observed and learned from African hunters. It's an art concerning which the western man, in his rush to technology and industrialization, is less sensitive. The western man's ears and eyes and nose may be physiologically and neurologically capable of the reception and distinction of the same stimuli perceivable to the African hunter, but these stimuli are simply not meaningful. The occidental may know the significance of a fine line on a graph showing the quantitative value of, for instance, the rise and fall of the stock market last week (about which the African hunter has no knowledge or interest). But he is utterly incapable of picking up the scent of roan antelope at a hundred yards on a slight breeze, calculating his distance from an elephant herd by the temperature of their manure, or making out the faint outline of a leopard flattened motionless

against a tree branch in the shadows of dusk. In the tropics, survival itself may depend upon the native's superior
intelligence and years of experience in reading all of these
signs. There is, however, no intelligence test standardized
and computerized to evaluate this vital life-or-death ability.

The experienced archeologist seems to be able to find
arrowheads lying on top of the ground that the average
archeological student would overlook because he doesn't
yet know what to ignore. Yet, the archeologist might not
be able to tell him the exact cues that made the image of
the arrowhead stand out so clearly. Edward T. Hall, in his
book, *The Hidden Dimension*, confirms what many of us
have known for a long time: women and men seem to
inhabit different visual worlds. A man cannot understand
why his wife is not able to comprehend the internal work-
ings of an automatic transmission or even to find the jack
handle in the trunk. Yet to him the inside of a refrigerator
continues to be a jungle and she must come and point out
where the cheese or leftover roast is hiding (often in front
of his eyes).[1] These differences in use of the eyes cannot be
attributed to the eyes' physical acuity. It seems that men
and women have just learned to use their eyes in different
ways.

*Double Image* is an attempt to show how cultural values
and differing world views inevitably affect interpretation
of scripture, especially passages that evoke theological dis-
cussion. Those who hold that the scriptures can be translated and proclaimed "culture free" are simply naive. These
pages, however, will not utilize the growing body of
knowledge from Christian anthropologists and cross-cultural communicators in a negative manner, as if only to point
up the weaknesses and limitations of western theological
interpretation filters. It will mean, however, that while
contrasting the wide disparity between North
American/European perceptual fields and those of West
Africans—some westerners might take offense. This is not
the author's intention. In no way do I wish to imply that

African culture is, by itself, a superior matrix from which to interpret scripture in an overarching generalization. This book wants to suggest that the agrarian and less industrialized environments of West African readers render them more closely akin to the original biblical speakers and hearers. I submit that the overall intent of these pages be seen as a paradigm for interpretation methodology—and not an overarching superior interpretation. I would trust that some scholars, theological students, clergy, and interested lay persons would find this approach to hermeneutics very comfortable. I recognize that others would find it equally disturbing. Consequently, these pages will try to show, in a positive vein, how the Holy Spirit inspires understanding of eternal truths for some third world brothers by employing their own cultural filters. And if we listen in as they hear and interpret the parables and other texts, we can learn with them. We will concentrate on West Africa, and specifically on the Mossi of Burkina Faso and the Ewe of Togo whose languages the author has learned.

In the spectrum of audible sound perceived by the human ear, only sound waves at frequencies from about 50 to 15,000 cycles per second can be heard. The sound spectrum of the human ear is really quite limited in relation to the total potential sound available. Many sound frequencies, especially on the higher range, are inaudible to man but perceptible to some animals, such as birds, dogs, and crickets. On the other hand, bullfrogs can croak at low frequencies equally inaudible to the human ear. In fact, one could say that there are "unheard melodies" that exist outside the human range of perception. Audibly we are prisoners of our hearing limitations just as we are encapsulated by the social and cultural limitations of our minds. (This is true of West Africans, of course, as well as North Americans.)

Because of this encapsulation, the words of Christ in his parables and his teachings seem to be saying different things to people in different cultures. Isn't it possible that he is saying things that we from the west do not hear because of industrialization and technology? We marvel at the Eskimo who can navigate for 100 miles across visually undifferentiated wasteland during a "white-out." Significant signs from the direction and smell of the wind together with the feel of the ice and snow under his feet provide cues that enable him to find his way. This book intends to give glimpses into scriptural understanding and illumination that the author himself could not see until aided by the world view and filter of African society and through Holy Spirit-enabled African minds.

The senses of the African hunter on the great savannah or the perception of the Eskimo in the frozen north shows us that eyes and ears are used differently. Christ said: "Who hath ears to hear, let him hear." Then he berated those who had closed the eyes and ears of their heart and had thus excluded themselves from understanding. Addressing his disciples Jesus added, "But blessed are your eyes because they see, and your ears because they hear" (Matthew 13:16).

In that optimistic spirit of positive intention, let us look at what some Africans can teach us.

### Notes

1. E.T. Hall, *The Hidden Dimension* (Garden City: Doubleday and Company, 1969), p. 105.

# Preface

"The media are western" is an accusation currently being leveled at western news reporters.

We are living in a time when the third world has organized an association of journalists and newscasters to represent what they feel is a legitimate gripe of having no *counter-penetration* in the media. Much of the two-thirds world and certainly African nations feel that they are victims of the media of western industrialized nations who interpret all events in Africa through western materialistic eyes and western political filters. They accuse the west of overemphasizing side issues in African news events, and neglecting the elements that the Africans themselves deem essential for understanding the "balanced wholeness" of a news event.

Is there not a chance of needing counter-penetration in biblical interpretation? Must the West African always depend on western cultural filters for his hermeneutic? Does not the traditional lifestyle of Africa's developing nations often more closely parallel the original context of the scriptures than does the North American lifestyle?

Why must a Togolese become an "intellectual westerner" before being given credit for having knowledge concerning Christian theology? I submit that this is the same fight the apostle Paul fought when in his epistles he blasted his own Jewish Christian brothers who insisted that the

Gentiles first become Jews before becoming Christian. Now, I believe there *is* such a thing as "biblical theology." I also subscribe to the belief that there ideally is a "supra-culture" which could release us from some of the cultural bondage of the west *or* the east. Note: Though my thesis will build a case for looking at West African culture to better understand *some* aspects of theology and biblical interpretation, by no means do I wish to suggest that *all* of African culture is superior or even, in all cases, a better filter to understand biblical truth. Much of West African culture *must* be *confronted* and modified by scripture, as should much of western secular culture. But for the west to think that the culture of the kingdom is Aristotelian, linear, industrialized, or materialistically and mathematically logical is a brand of the old cultural and ecclesiastical imperialism under which the foreign church has suffered and still is suffering.

## Contextualization

The central issue before those who interpret scripture in these days of our rapidly becoming a "global village" is certainly going to be the question of revelation and culture. Those who argue that revelation is not enculturated but is "pure" and totally predictable will fall into the same error Adolf Julicher did in 1886. In combating the rampant Augustinian "allegorism" of his day, he overreacted to an extreme position perhaps few would hold today. He proclaimed that every parable has *one* and *only one* central point. Julicher's cultural mentality or "mental grid" simply could not allow the ambiguity that Christ did intend.

The African stories and parables in this book each lead to an amplification or clarification of scriptural passages. They illustrate how precision itself, from a cultural orientation, is sometimes a trap which leads to poor interpretation or misunderstanding of God's intent.

Archibald Hunter interestingly notes that parables comprise more than one-third of Jesus' recorded teaching, and he proceeds to give us an excellent work on the parables of Jesus. Yet Mr. Hunter is a prime example of a typical western thinker who cannot believe that Jesus meant to be ambiguous in Mark 4 or in Matthew 13, and does not see how Jesus could have uttered words to deliberately hide truth. How sad to hear the author say, "It is worth observing that great parables are evidently so difficult to create that it is hard to name another person in history with more than one or two good ones to his credit."[1] Here, then, is proof that counter-penetration into western religious thought is sorely needed. Mr. Hunter simply is not aware of a great portion of the world who think and talk in parables in their everyday speech. How sad that the cunning minds of the Mossi, for example, have never touched his life. There thousands of ordinary individuals as well as leaders in society are still creating great parables. To explain it simply, the increasing need for precision in a technological world has resulted in an intolerance for the ambiguity of parabolic or enigmatic ways of considering information. And when the traditional world of developing countries speaks artistically and indirectly, it's not only the media that do not hear; the western church, too, hardly pays attention.

Writing on what Jesus really meant in his parables, Thieliche and Jeremias and Wallace all exemplify the western "Germanic-Anglo grid" that seems to have no capacity to evaluate an aural/oral world view as held by pre-literate peoples. I cite Mr. Hunter here again, not to take harsh exception to his insight (I personally like him better than most others), but because he typifies the insensitivity to the point of view which this book espouses. Hunter states that the parable of the laborers (Matthew, chapter 20) has had something added. He implies that the church is at fault for the inclusion of verse 16: "So the last shall be first, and the first last." In the appendix Hunter says, "This saying really misses the point. The parable teaches no lesson about the reversal of rank at the end, since all laborers received precisely the same wage."[2] Is it because he, Hunter, and others find the ambiguity untenable? Is it common practice by western thinkers to *suppose* something amiss with the text, or the translators, every time the meaning becomes difficult for their own world view of acceptable, logical thought processes? "Misses the point"? I submit that this *is* the point of the parable. This is the *second agenda* that the west refuses to consider because that thinking pattern is outside of its perception. This is where Africans can help us! West African culture, not obsessed with a "quantification" which blocks understanding to another dimension, gives us a cultural perspective that facilitates *seeing* and *hearing*.

I find it regrettable that some commentators on the story of the talents in Matthew 25 suggest that verse 29 has also been "added on." Some even state that in its present context, verse 29 tears apart the other verses in the account. Absolutely amazing! As if there could be nothing wrong with "my" thought processes. As if there must *certainly* be something wrong with the translator or copier!

What a joy it would be to see someone write words such as, "Do you suppose there is something about our thinking processes that does not allow us to see clearly here?" Immediately attacking the translator or the church fathers for adding something when one finds a passage unclear is tantamount to kicking the neighbor's dog when you're frustrated with your own children or household.

These are some of the reasons I have determined that this book needs to be written. Africans have enriched my life immeasurably. They have taught me to see in a different dimension. They have taught me that *process* is more important than *product*. From the edge of the Sahara, people have opened my mind to the potential of another orientation. They remind me that holy scripture is essentially an eastern book and not a western book.

African indirect speaking with parables and legends and sayings has the capacity to coax us to discover something new! Their mode of communication can help us better understand the scriptures by leading us to a spontaneous moment of insight. Allegory can allow mental space (time) and a choice, permitting one to participate personally in the event. Thus one can reach back and touch a traditional culture and perhaps, just perhaps, arrive at a meaning that the Holy Spirit can make relevant for our own day.

## Timing and Reading

Some people may profit from this book by reading a chapter in isolation and not reading the whole as one would a novel. Modern life is like that—small segments that seemingly stand independently. The twentieth century tends to cause us to compartmentalize our lives, because that's the nature of a technological age. And we sometimes need to compartmentalize our lives for protection from our changing society. Some people may want to read a chapter by itself, in prayerful meditation, so as to make its lesson relevant to the occasion of that day or time frame. Often it's very beneficial to ponder one idea and weigh it over a period of time without confusing it or diluting it with other competing ideas. (Not that ideas and new thoughts should never have competition—far from it. In fact, just the opposite is necessary in some contexts.) But it is good to expose oneself to an idea long enough for the potential of that idea to have an effect, like exposing oneself to the sun for a suntan (if you're a Caucasian and you happen to think that a darker shade of skin has social benefits). In our search for God and his power and direction in our lives, we

1. **Traditional African Telegraph.**

sometimes pursue him best by giving him opportunity to pursue us through "exposure time" to his word.

These little stories and thoughts contain quite a variety of ideas. Some of them may be too controversial to be assimilated by everyone. It is my intent to *overstate* occasionally because that seems to be the only way to get some people's attention. I would hope that the reader will not make the mistake that some people make with fish. Some people never eat them because of the bones. Can a thousand year old culture contribute to biblical clarity?

This book is written in the hope that the reader will tolerate some new ideas for the duration, and get as much of the fish meat as possible.

## Parabolic and Narrative Speaking

*Gwom gwomda ne a pagedo—Bi a yam soaba yaolen wegese.*

(Words are spoken with their peelings/shells. Let the wise person come to shuck them.) Here is a Mossi proverb from West Africa that introduces well the topic of parabolic and narrative speech that, having been lost for centuries in the West, has only recently begun to gain respect.

Public speakers have a new interest in using narrative communication. For over 1,500 years, preaching has been characterized by analytical rhetoric in style and presentation. This resulted from the influence of the Hellenistic world. The early church forged its tools of propagation, not from the Hebrew world of its founding, but the Greco-Roman culture that first persecuted it and then embraced it. The narrative and often indirect style of parable and story that characterized the first-century church carried the imprint of the Hebrew synagogue.[3]

When the church moved into the social/political orbit of Greek thinking, a more analytical straightforward approach ensued. In his introduction to *Preaching Biblically*, Don Wardlaw states:

> When the church moved solidly into the Hellenistic world to offer the gospel, however, preaching adopted a discursive style that only now is being seriously reconsidered in contrast to first century narrative preaching, reflection became the basic sermon framework in the second century...church fathers from Origen to Chrysostom, while imbued with the mind of Christ, exegeted and preached with the mind of Plato and Aristotle.[4]

Wardlaw continues by saying that though Black preaching has been the notable exception in the United States, most American preachers have modeled their preaching on the sermon as argument—as if in a court of law. He lightly chides public speakers who have little success in breaking the dominance of the Cartesian grid. "The Greeks have stolen into Homiletical Troy and still reign."[5] But there has been a significant change in recent years, as the discipline of communications theory enlightens scholars to the fresh research data on human cognition itself.

Public speakers in the west are beginning to see the value and power of using what our African-American brothers and sisters have long known to be effective—utilizing first-person narratives, parables, similes, or stories to carry the freight of the intended content. Seminaries are finally beginning to take a cue from the social sciences and to shift from the almost exclusive fixation with content when teaching homiletical skills. They now also recognize the importance of the intended audience as an important factor in preaching and teaching. Focusing on human perception and audience-centered speaking will raise the paramount question: What kind of communication will be the best remembered and have the most impact?

Ralph Lewis, professor of preaching at Asbury Theological Seminary, has written a very interesting (and rather non-academic) book, *Learning to Preach Like Jesus*, in which he tells of an African student of his who was given advice before coming to America. "Go to America and learn to preach like the white man preaches," his denominational leaders admonished him. "Don't come back here telling stories like the untrained tribal preachers and the Pentecostals do."[6] Western preachers, in general, have never been taught to let a narrative style carry the central theme of a sermon. Our seminaries, generally, confine the use of stories in a sermon to illustrations that serve as amplification of the "superior" mode of Aristotelian rhetoric.

The above Mossi proverb relating to "words used with their peelings" speaks of a recognition on the part of this people that speech has a dimension or texture rather like a "thickness." This writer's research on West African speech mannerisms during dissertational work for the University of Minnesota included Africans who had been educated in Europe. They encouraged looking past what the ordinary "European" sees to find deep significance in both the style and content of the two-thirds world speech understanding.

It's only when you open the shell of words and begin to look down inside the shell at the nut that the words have dimension and feeling and texture. The white man does not think that the outside peeling has any value and so he goes directly for the nut and uses the nut (as in a peanut) thinking that the outside shuck or shell is useless. Our proverb says that the shell (the part the European often discards) is as important as the nut of the word, because it brings balance and perspective to what a person wants to say. It also takes a skillful person to know when to believe the shell or when to believe the nut or what proportion of each one in a mixture should be used for the circumstance in question. Often, Europeans use naked words. We feel that using the nut of a word without the shell is using the word as if it were naked. The naked words can cause injury (sometimes not intended) by the European and his manner of speaking.[7]

Professor Lewis' student quoted above confirms this. "Despite the advice I received before coming to America, I have come to see that story telling and narrative preaching may be closer to Jesus' practice than most Western preaching is and I know from experience it surely comes much closer to the hearts of my people."[8]

This writer's intent is to illustrate how the traditional West African mind can contribute greatly to the West's understanding of scripture. Perhaps the perceptive reader may also find a good model with which to enlarge his/her communication skills.[9]

### Notes

1. Archibald Hunter, *Interpreting the Parables* (Philadelphia: Westminster Press, 1960), p. 104.
2. Ibid., p. 216.
3. See Robert C. Worley, *Preaching and Teaching in the Earliest Church* (Westminster Press, 1979). Also: Dewitteh Holland, *The Preaching Tradition: A Brief History* (Abingdon Press, 1988).
4. Don M. Wardlaw, ed., *Preaching Biblically* (Westminster Press, 1983), p. 11.
5. Ibid, pp. 12 and 13.
6. Ralph Lewis, *Learning to Preach Like Jesus* (Westchester, Illinois: Crossway Books, 1989), p. 25.
7. Daniel Pasgo, as quoted in Del Tarr, *Indirection and Ambiguity as a Mode of Communication in West Africa* (unpublished Ph.D. dissertation, University of Minnesota, 1979), p. 143.
8. Lewis, op. cit., p. 25.

9.  Some readers may wish to pursue the hypothesis that the Hebrew and the two-thirds world (that has not yet been infected by Aristotle) are better suited to understanding some of scripture. See also Brad Young's work, *Jesus and His Jewish Parables: Rediscovering the Roots of Jesus' Teaching* (New York: Paulist Press, 1989).

# 1

# Double Image/
# African Insight

I trust you have read the introduction and preface as they
will add much to clarity. I am attempting a difficult task in
communications. This difficulty has less to do with you the
reader than with me the source. The cultural bridge to West
African thinking we are hoping to cross is an exciting
adventure, but it is not without its perils. This is especially
true for the "literalist." That's the person who believes it's
always possible to arrive at exact, precise meanings in all
human dialogue. He/she seldom ever goes to see live drama,
for example, because of the difficulty in understanding
imagery. Some people do not enjoy the energy required to
play the game of symbolism.

I would love to be an artist and be able to draw cartoons,
especially political and religious cartoons! In a symbolic
way, *Double Image* from African thinking is an attempt to
draw mental pictures. All Africans are verbal cartoonists.
And in the Bible Jesus too shows a great sense of humor
himself[1] in many of his parables and dialogue. I would hope
this book would increase the reader's appreciation for
Jesus' parables which represent over 37% of his recorded
words.

There is a teaching method called "guided discovery" of which I strongly approve. Briefly, guided discovery is a way of bringing a student to discover for him/herself the truth wished to be imparted by the teacher or the answer to a question posed by the teacher. What we can discover for ourselves we never forget! Sometimes teachers give too many answers and it's no wonder some of us don't retain much after the final exam! The great value of guided discovery is that it is heuristic; not only is the element being taught being discovered, but many other related and even parallel ideas and truths have a good chance of becoming a part of the reader's or student's perception as well.

Some of the publishers to whom I sent chapters of this book wrote back that they thought I was expecting too much of a North American audience by not giving more cues or hints about the many African stories, parables and aphorisms in the text. This presented me with a dilemma. If I gave too many cues and introductions such as this, then I would be spoiling the element of discovery. As one perceptive author says: "The trouble with most books about humor is, they get it down and break its arm."[2] Of course that is not only the problem with humor; it's also the problem with parables. If the teller explains everything, then the punch line is rather spoiled.

Nonetheless, I will faithfully give a little warm-up or setting before each chapter. I promise in so doing not to spoil your discovery. I have great confidence in human intelligence and in the joy that you the reader too will find in both understanding the message intended *and* the many insights you are going to receive on your own. This will be especially true for those readers who can take a step back from seeking always a quick literal meaning.

In this chapter, "Double Image/African Insight," three stories are included to set the tone for subsequent chapters. This chapter specifically contains an explanation of farming methods not known in North America. In *Why the Sower Weeps,* it gives African insight into why a farmer would sow grain while weeping as suggested in Psalm 126. We'll also explore a very difficult passage in Matthew 13:12, *Ears To Hear,* which seems so extremely undemocratic that most westerners stumble over it. We'll also find out in *Hold It Lightly* how to hold an egg for anyone aspiring to be a leader or even a good parent.

"Double Image/African Insight" can best be explained by comparing the view of a faraway scene through a one lens telescope with that of a pair of binoculars. You get a clearer view when using both eyes. Of course one eye would represent looking at the Bible through North American culture and the other eye looking at the scriptures through West African culture. The reader should be careful not to interpret the book title *Double Image* to mean that the second image is necessarily going to make the scene to be a *different* one. When two eyes function properly they look in the same direction. The advantage of two eyes over one is depth perception, clarity, and added color.

## Why the Sower Weeps

I spent the first five years of my life on a farm in northern Minnesota. My father had a dairy farm with thoroughbred Holsteins, and used the old sling-type Surge milkers. He raised corn for silage and a few acres of cereal grains on the relatively rich bottomland on the banks of the Mississippi. This period of my life is represented by the house and the land—from where my earliest memories exist. My father was very affectionate with me, his first son, and I would accompany him while he would sow grain with a team of horses or do other farm work with one of the first tractors in the region. (I was deathly afraid of the sound of that Oliver Hart Par engine starting; but once it was running, I would ride in Dad's lap as he steered it.) I suppose all children are closely attuned to the emo-

## 2. Grinding Grain.

tions of their parents. I certainly was, but I don't recall my father ever weeping while he sowed grain. He was more apt to be whistling!

While on that land, my father experienced a religious conversion and felt called into the ministry. The family then moved to Minneapolis for his ministerial training. Subsequent years were spent in three different pastorates while I was going through primary and high school. These years were in small towns where most of the church people were farmers. I spent much time with the children of the deacons and other church families, and during those happy years I learned much about farming methods and farm machinery. I learned to drive John Deere, Case, and Farmall tractors for planting, cultivating, and harvesting the essential crops on which the farmers lived. But in all that time, I never once saw a farmer or any member of his family weep while sowing seeds. So, like most Americans, I didn't know what to think when reading a scripture text like Psalm 126:5-6:

> Those who sow in tears will reap with songs of joy.
> He who goes out weeping, carrying seed to sow, will
> return with songs of joy, carrying sheaves with him.

Many explanations and good analogies have been drawn from these verses and have been related by ministers to the process of witnessing and the gathering of converts. The seed has been likened to the word of God or the message about the kingdom that Christ talked about in his parable of the sower in Matthew 13. These are all good and reasonable and valid explanations, but I still had never seen someone weep while planting, nor had I ever heard anyone witnessing that phenomenon—until my own family lived in West Africa on the great Sahel. This semi-arid bush country stretches in a narrow band between the Sahara Desert and the tropical rain forest on the coast. This savannah country receives from 20 to 40 inches of rain a year, but all of it falls in a very short period during the four months from May to August. A year's supply of food must be raised in that short growing season. The eight month dry season which follows the rain represents some of the most severe weather conditions of any inhabited region on the globe. The following scene is indelibly etched on my memory. It does not represent an exceptional drought year (they are even worse), but is a fair description of an event that takes place in thousands of families every year. Let's set the stage:

Harvest time is a joyous time on the savannah in West Africa, because food is in abundance. People can smile and laugh and there is much dancing far into the night as the African in his traditional ceremonies gives thanks to the "creator" and "sustainer." The "creator god" is seen as the male and earth as the female, who has again given of her abundance in fertility.

The staple crop all across the savannah is millet, and from this a meal is ground to make mush which is eaten twice a day during the months of plenty (October, November, and December). The main meal of the day, eaten just before retiring, is a happy time, about 7:00 p.m. People sleep well on a full stomach. About January, these two meals become smaller, as the granary is noticeably diminished from its original bounty. Then for many families, the month of February brings quite a change in eating habits. To conserve grain until the next rainfall, they permit themselves only one main meal, which is still eaten each day at bedtime. (In traditional Africa, obesity was the luxury of only the royal lineage.)

April and May are the saddest months of the year. Many families are running out of food. It is not unusual to hear, in the hush of an African dusk, small babies and young children crying from real, physical hunger, as well as from discouraging prospects that the day's one meal will satisfy the gnawing pains in their tummies. What does a father or mother say to a six-year-old boy who, after eating the only meal of the day, looks up and says, "Daddy, I'm still hungry"?

In the last few weeks before the new rains come, bringing new hope and also some quick-growing new vegetable crops, many families sell some of their dearest possessions to buy a few handfuls of grain to keep them alive. Many wives boil bark and roots from trees and certain plants to be able to give the family something at the end of the day. It is difficult to adequately describe the barrenness and desolation of a landscape that has not had rain for eight months under the broiling tropical sun!

During this time when the majority of the population is on the edge of disaster, some bright-eyed boy will come running to his father with the joyous exclamation, "Daddy, Daddy, we've got some grain! Quickly, take it to Mommie so she can make us some mush, so tonight our tummies can be quiet."

The father asks, "Son, where did you find the grain?"

The little boy answers, "You know, in the extra hut over by the animal corral. Inside there is a leather pouch and it has grain in it!"

The father has to explain to the son that this is seed grain for next year's crop and is the only hope between them and starvation. Yes, it does belong to them, but they dare not eat it. The father, too, has been thinking of that grain as he watches the tummies of his children distend from malnutrition and

## 3. Weeping Sower.

notes in himself and in his wife the vastly reduced level of energy due to the same lack of protein. This is a time of year when ordinary diseases, that the body would normally throw off, claim many lives.

When the first rains come and the hard cracked ground begins to soften, the whole family goes to the field in their weakened condition. With great effort they clear the fields and get them ready for planting. I've seen it time and time again, where the father will take down that leather sack, and with tears in his eyes, literally throw away and bury the very commodity that the bodies of every member of his household desperately need. He weeps because he is sorry for the delay between planting and harvest. Oh, if one only dared to eat it. In spite of that sorrow, he plants it—he invests it in Mother Nature. He has faith in the harvest! He weeps now; he believes he can dance and sing later.

I have heard African preachers take this text and make this analogy to an audience of hearers who did not need the above explanation. I have heard them say: "Unless you and I are willing to take something which is rightfully ours (with which we can do anything we desire because it is ours), and plant it, and invest it—we don't really understand the passage." Listen to these bush preachers say: "If we haven't wept over the things that we hold most dear, then we have probably never 'sown in tears.'"

If your and my efforts for the sake of God's kingdom come from an affluent economic structure so that our giving (whether of time or material things) does not really affect our immediate lifestyle—doesn't *cost* us anything in personal deprivation—then how can we confidently look forward to rejoicing and "bringing our sheaves with us"? I think Africans are right. Doesn't it seem reasonable that the Christ who taught his disciples about those who throw into the treasury from their abundance, in contrast to the widow's mite, might still be watching for those whose giving *hurts*? How much—or what—would it take for the average North American to "sow in tears"? The promise is clear. We can only expect to laugh at harvest time if we have been willing to weep at planting time. This is another one of God's paradoxes in the scriptures that contains great victory, blessing, and largeness of life. There are no doubt other good explanations of this passage. I happen to believe the people on the great African savannah have a very good one that is related to their ecological system. It has spiritual implications for us all. May God grant us spiritual eyes to see.

I tell you the truth, unless a kernel of wheat falls to the ground and dies, it remains only a single seed. But if it dies it produces many seeds (John 12:24).

## Ears to Hear

The class was overhead to interrupt their teacher with the question: "Why do you speak to the people in parables?" The teacher had just finished talking to them about the sower, the parables of the weeds, the mustard seed, and yeast and leaven. His response was:

The knowledge of the secrets of the kingdom of heaven has been given to you, but not to them. Whoever has will be given more, and he will have an abundance. Whoever does not have, even what he has will be taken from him (Matthew 13:11-12).

People who live in our democratic systems have great difficulty with verse 12 because it is so extremely undemocratic. We believe in equality, and this verse seems to ignore an ideal about sharing and underdogs and such things. The ancient teacher continued:

Though seeing, they do not see; though hearing, they do not hear or understand. In them is fulfilled the prophecy of Isaiah: "You will be ever hearing but never understanding; you will be ever seeing but never perceiving. For this people's heart has become calloused; they hardly hear with their ears, and they have closed their eyes. Otherwise they might see with their eyes, hear with their ears, understand with their hearts and turn, and I would heal them" (Matthew 12:13-15).

"Now," you say, "isn't that the gospel's intent? Didn't Jesus want to heal and bless everybody? Doesn't the church proclaim 'whosoever will'? It fits so neatly with democracy and equality."

How can one justify the apparent contradiction? The Master is plainly saying he would *exclude* some from his blessing. Centuries ago from across the Atlantic came our conceptual, logical Aristotelian based method of cognition. It serves us well and is good. Much of life in our world would be chaotic without our "conceptual systems." But as much as I first resisted it I must now admit that the conceptual thinking of the west isn't universally appreciated nor sometimes useful to understand some scriptural truths (like this Matthew 13 passage). Edmund Perry talks about ways of thinking in North America that are assumed to be universally valid:

We Western Christians, in particular, need to be shocked out of our unexamined reverence for logical concepts. There is nothing uniquely Christian or sacrosanct about logical concepts and we ought to be prepared to explore the possibility of understanding and communicating the gospel in other than logical conceptual categories.[3]

Listen to this West African story that I believe can illustrate the hard-to-understand verses in Matthew 13.

There was a man who had two sons: The older son did
not obey his father. He sometimes even criticized his
father. This made the father very sad. The younger son
obeyed his dad. In fact, he would often go the second
mile. The father would ask him to do something and
he would say, "Yes, Father"; and he wouldn't just do
what his father asked, but he would do extra.

Now in his tribal culture, it is very common for a
father to make arrangements with a family outside his
own endogamous (or closed) family for a "daughter"
(a very young girl to be brought into his family). He
will raise this girl as his own daughter, knowing full
well that this "daughter" will eventually become the
wife of one of his sons. (Thus marriage in much of the
world is not a contract between two people, but a
contract between two families.)

So, this man made arrangements for a young girl,
about eight, to be brought to the family. She didn't
take the role of a wife. She began to learn the ways of
that family. The sons watched this girl as she grew up
and became a beautiful girl—not just beautiful to look
at, but beautifully natured. Both of the young men
(the obedient younger son and the disobedient older
son) wanted her.

As the years passed, the girl matured emotionally and
physically and was ready to be married according to
African custom. Every time the father thought about
giving her to the older son he felt sad—"This boy does
not obey me. This boy sometimes calls me a fool." And
every time he thought about giving her to the younger

one, his heart was filled with joy. "This is the one who deserves her," he thought.

When he would mention these thoughts to his "family," about which son would marry the daughter, he would say: "I don't want to give her to the older one. He's not a good son. I want to give her to the younger one. He's the good son." But his brothers and uncles would say: "Oh, it is not our custom. You must never give a wife to the younger son without first giving a wife to the older son." So he let this decision wait for many months. Finally he knew what he was going to do.

He waited until one very dark night while it was raining (no moon, no stars). In the middle of the night he got up, went to the sleeping girl, awakened her, and took her out in the middle of this hard rain to the sleeping quarters of his sons. (In African custom, adult sons each have a separate hut or sleeping room.) So he went to the older son's hut, clapped, and said: "Is my older son there?"

His older son woke up: "Father, what do you want?"

The father called in a loud voice to make certain his son would hear: "I have a young thing here and I do not want water to get in its ears that it should die. Please come and take it into your hut."

The older son called out: "Father, you old fool, what are you doing out in the rain? Take that thing back to your own hut and leave me alone—I'm sleeping."

The father went to the younger son's hut, clapped, and said: "Is my younger son there?"

The younger son woke up: "Hey, Father, what are you doing in this rain? Why didn't you just call me from your hut? What are you doing standing out there?"

So the father said the same thing. "I have a young thing here and I do not want water to get in its ears that it should die. Please come and take it into your hut."

The young son quickly opened the door, came out in the middle of the night, and said: "Father, why didn't you just call me from your hut? I would have come over there and saved you the trouble."

Now in the complete darkness, the father put the hand of the beautiful young girl into the hand of the younger son. He felt around and realized that it was this girl, and he gave a whoop of joy because he knew what had happened! He'd just been given a wife! When the older son heard the commotion, he called out, "What's the commotion out there?"

The young son called back, "Dad has just given me a wife!"

The disciples asked the teacher: "Why do you speak to people in parables?" What do you think?

The father in the story above now had an excuse for why he hadn't obeyed local custom. When all of his uncles and brothers would come and say, "Why did you do this?" he could say, "I offered her to my older son and he refused."

Someday the heavenly Father may ask Jesus, "What about these who are not in the kingdom?" And he'll reply, "Oh, I gave them an opportunity and they refused." Should it really be so hard a scripture for us to understand? Jesus is so clearly indicating, "There are some people I want to

## 4. Traditional African Village.

exclude because they have already closed their eyes and ears. They have been practicing it."
Consider verse 12:

Whoever has will be given more, and he will have an abundance. Whoever does not have, even what he has will be taken from him.

Remember that poor, miserable, fearful servant (in Matthew 25) who took his one talent and buried it? It was taken from him—*even that which he had.* And look whom it was given to—not the one with four, but the guy with ten! Now, there is no equality in that!

Jesus turned to his disciples and said, "Blessed are your eyes, for they see. Blessed are your ears, for they hear." Think of how the Spirit strives with us to get us to do something about our will—not just once, but a daily conscious alignment of our will and faith-life toward God that sets a posture of Christian behavior. It's cumulative. The scores of right decisions that we make every day, every week, every year, add up to a posture which someday will allow us to hear the intent of his parable-like words. He has so designed it. Christ will not have habitual "wrong-decision-makers" inherit his kingdom. And he will find a way to exclude them and still be able to say to the Father, "See, I offered it to them, but they had already closed their ears and their eyes." These rebellious ones may have had a legal right to a blessing like the older son in the story. But through the posturing made by the composite of hundreds of wrong decisions, they excluded themselves.

God has fixed the rules. *The person who is self-centered, self-destructs.*

Think back—"I have this little thing here and I don't want water to get in its ears that it should die." "Go away, you fool." Or: "Father, why didn't you just call to me from your hut? I would have come out and gotten the little thing."

I want to be a disciple that hears Christ's words: "Blessed are *your* eyes, for they see, and *your* ears, for they hear."

## Hold It Lightly

If God at any time should decide to inhibit mankind's bent to sin by preventing people from sinning with some visible spectacle of power, he would totally destroy the freedom of the human will. The consequence would render all human goodness an impossibility. So, God leaves the freedom of man's will untouched. It must be that way.

Created in God's image (with the power to create), man has been entrusted with the freedom to choose his own spiritual destiny. Not only that, he has also been given the responsibility to decide how he will present himself (in interpersonal relations) to other members of Christ's church—especially as that relates to personal power, status, and social influence. The Ashanti of Ghana know that man's search for piety and personal power are related. Even before becoming Christians they understood Matthew 6:1 (RSV), where Christ says: "Beware of practicing your piety before men in order to be seen by them." The Ashanti know that Christ completely rejects the *bronze plaque* mentality about the giving of alms either for attention or as an abuse of personal power and influence for selfish reasons.

It is interesting to note in the gospels how the disciples were repeatedly plagued with status and power problems. They completely misunderstood Christ's "kingdom" which he was about to establish. We read the gospels and criticize the disciples for squabbling about who would be the greatest. Neither the disciples then nor today's church seems to see that Christ is proposing an order in which the question of status is rendered irrelevant. Let's come to our small Ashanti proverb:

The responsibility of power is like holding an egg. Grasp it too tightly and it will drip through your fingers; hold it too loosely and it will drop and break.

I do not question the teaching of the New Testament as to the necessary existence of leaders and administrators in the body of Christ. Their existence is clearly logical and consistent with God's nature and revelation. But why, why has each succeeding revival through church history been first a move away from a clergy-dominated church back to a "laymen's movement," only to end again in a clergy-dominated religious structure? Why is it that, when the goal of our seminaries and Bible colleges is stated to be one of training shepherds and servants, they are producing kings? What is there about the human spirit that militates toward territoriality—a bent for power—and leads to exclusivism, legalism, and religious imperialism? Here, then, is the scripture that the African's "egg" seeks to clarify:

In the world, kings lord over their subjects; and those in authority are called their country's benefactors. Not so with you: on the contrary, the highest among you must bear himself like the youngest; the chief of you, like a servant. For who is greater—the one who sits at table or the servant who waits on him? Surely the one who sits at table. Yet here am I among you like a servant (Luke 2:24-27, NEB).

Who can doubt that this is highly revolutionary doctrine? It has not yet been taken seriously—even by the church. Talk to the man on the street representing the unchurched majority in North America, and he will tell you that he is sick to death of the eternal wrangling of the clergy and those "religions."

In life and death Jesus didn't squeeze *or* drop the egg. We must learn to exemplify him. He brought unto himself a circle of disciples who came from diverse types of peo-

## 5. Holding the Egg.

ple. They were not acceptable to the clergy of their day and would be welcome in few religious societies today. Yet their souls (though transparently weak and imperfect) eventually caught the lesson. History records how they "turned the world upside down" by paying the ultimate price—while still holding the egg lightly.

A young preacher came to me, disillusioned about his denomination. He spoke wistfully of the pattern he saw in the New Testament, where clergy and laity were much less distinguishable than what he felt had happened in his own denomination. He talked of the days of its early beginnings, which he felt adhered much closer to the New Testament pattern. He asked some very hard questions with tears in his voice. He asked how a denomination could start out as a "laymen's movement" and then in a few short decades develop into a "preacher movement" when the original reason for being was a move away from a clergy-dominated structure back to a definition of the priesthood of the believer. He wondered how his leaders could equate "success" only with honor and power. What administrative evolution prevailed that professional clergy could become more interested in "keeping shop" and "keeping rules" than in touching and healing sin-sick souls?

Ashanti Christians think that Jesus knew about the balance required between the two extremes of manipulation of power as suggested by the egg proverb. To be a leader, one must truly lead. If one cannot distinguish the difference between a leader and a follower, then the definition of "leader" is inappropriate. An absence of leadership is what the Ashanti see as letting the egg fall to break on the ground.

The other extreme of leadership is exemplified by the analogy of holding the egg too tightly, so that it is crushed by the muscles of the hand and fingers. These are the most readily identifiable examples, and we have been referring to them above. Life is full of sad pictures of mothers who in the name of "love" hold on to their children too tightly, never allowing them breathing room to mature. Mother thinks she is really loving them when in actuality she is over-controlling them. An African can do it, an administrator in a school, or a teacher in the classroom—anyone who must constantly remind others that she/he is superior is *squeezing* the egg.

Here is the nub of meaning to Christ's words when he said, "Save it and you will lose it. Be willing to lose it and paradoxically you will save it" (see Mark 8:35). Hold the egg lightly, but not too lightly; firmly, but not too firmly. Mankind generally seeks power. God gives it to those who *could* seek it but won't. It's God's law that works inexorably in his kingdom. He who is self-centered, self-destructs.

If you really want to know the mark of a person—to know whether that person has internal maturity, self-confidence, and integrity of character—give the *advantage* and see what he/she does with it. Do you know someone quick to "cash in" on all of his or her rights? If you do, you probably have seen someone with yellow yolk running off the elbow!

Moses had the chance of a lifetime. God was speaking to him and said, "I'll make you a great nation—step aside, Moses. I'll destroy those rebellious sinners and start over again with you" (see Exodus 32:9-10). Moses didn't squeeze the egg. Nor did he drop it. Abraham too handled the egg just right in the episode of sacrificing his son Isaac as an act of obedience to God. And Christ showed us how to hold the egg when Satan said to him, "I'll give you all of this if you..." or when he was nailed to the cross and taunts came to him, "Come down from the cross if you are the son of God..."

Jesus knew that *coming up* from the tomb was more powerful than *coming down* from the cross.

Hundreds of years of African culture have taught its people much wisdom to understand great principles in the scriptures. Don't squeeze the egg.

*Notes*

1. For a different view of Jesus of Nazareth see Elton Trueblood, *The Humor of Christ* (New York: Harper and Row, 1964).
2. James Thurber, as quoted in Don Wardlaw, ed., *Preaching Biblically* (Philadelphia: The Westminster Press, 1983), p. 15.
3. Edmund Perry, *The Gospel in Dispute* (Garden City: Doubleday, 1958), p. 101.

# 2

# Difficult Passages Illuminated

Need I remind the reader that the Bible is an eastern book? Westerners generally don't like the idea. Most theology in the world as we know it has strong western cultural overtones. The west after all was the part of the world that accepted Christianity most readily and sent missionaries with great fervor to every other continent. Nonetheless, the culture of the Bible is really very different from even the parent cultures of western societies, not to mention the mechanistic, materialistic, consumer-dominated societies we see in modern North America. So, it shouldn't come as a surprise that older cultures like Africa and Asia would contain in them examples, allegories, and lessons which would illuminate parts of the Bible which our own world view and social structure might obscure. We began to illustrate this concept in the previous chapter from the story of the two sons related to Matthew 13:12.

In this chapter we will discuss some of the very words of Jesus that surprise some and confuse others. Is it possible that we can find something from Africa (*Eyes of an Old Man*) that would help the dilemma of Jesus' actions and words in John's gospel, chapter eight? Here a woman was brought before him who had actually been caught in the act of adultery. How could he have been so lenient? Some Bible interpreters are a bit embarrassed by the fact that Jesus sided with the sinful woman and not the religious leaders who were accusing her. Let's look at other words of Jesus that are difficult to understand.

In Luke chapter nine, Jesus tells a would-be follower to "let the dead bury their dead." What could he possibly mean? So we'll consider two views of this seemingly difficult passage in *Christ the Fisherman* and *To Know But Not Show*.

Forgiveness is not a strong characteristic of any nation. North Americans are no better at it than anyone else. On this vital topic, so important to Jesus, we'll see in *Mane Sugri I and II* how an African language can semantically inform us about a characteristic that God made obligatory. And where does one find the balance between forgiveness and God's justice and retribution? Many people are confused with the idea that love can cover sins, and if love *does* cover sins then that poses a new difficulty. If sins are covered, how can confession take place which leads to repentance and ultimate forgiveness?

I would not be so bold as to write about these difficult topics if I claimed to have the ultimate answer (or even worse, the only answer or interpretation). I believe strongly that theology is in process. Western man has done an admirable job of interpreting scripture. However, in my view God's word will only have greater universal understanding when biblical interpretation from the west is joined by that of African, Asian, and Latin American expositors whose knowledge of the Bible's original languages can resonate through their own mental perception and cultural richness. (What a joy to see this process begin as the two-third's world scholars begin to emerge!) Examine with me, in this chapter, the added candlepower of illumination that African cultures bring.

# The Eyes of an Old Man

The first eleven verses of the eighth chapter of John tell an important story. Commentators cannot agree on its interpretation or the significance of its projected meaning; nor can they refrain from writing copious chapters of explanation on the subject of the woman taken in adultery—the very act. Some of these explanations are excellent and bring to light many facets of the culture in which Christ lived that are, indeed, profitable for any serious student. Perhaps it is Christ's pronouncement, "Neither do I condemn thee: go and sin no more," that so many have felt the need to explain. It seems so contrary to the clear indication in the scriptures about the penalty for adultery. Would that in the scriptures all human behavior was set off in such bold relief concerning its "rightness" or "wrongness" as is this act!

The setting was the temple, early in the morning, where Christ had come to teach those who gathered around him. In the middle of that class setting, the adulteress was introduced (no doubt in great disarray and much confusion) for the Pharisees' own type of "show and tell." They reminded the Master that the law of Moses commanded that she should be stoned for such an act. Then Jesus began to write in the sand—which action has inspired much speculation. The Pharisees continued to press Jesus for an answer, and he spoke to them about sinlessness and throwing stones, and he continued to write on the ground. The scene continued until everyone had left except the woman and Jesus surrounded by the original class members.

Very disturbing story, this! How do you tell this story—let alone explain it to a society wherein sexual sins have been blown way out of proportion to the neglect of others equally as desperate? I doubt that there is another society in which one can find so great a disparity between one segment of the population preoccupied with the consciousness of the *sinfulness* of the lusts of the flesh, and another large segment of that same society that *exploits* sex for its commercial and capitalistic gains. This is our own western society.

An African tale, told in Burkina Faso and Ghana and Nigeria (and perhaps in many more countries), in my opinion, clarifies this story and helps us examine some of Christ's possible motives for his disturbing behavior.

One day after school, some children were playing ball before going to their homes. There was a hungry old man who was passing by, and he thought that the school children would not see him catch a rooster near the school yard. The rooster did not belong to him, but he snatched it and put it in his bag. However, some of the school children did see him and started shouting, "There's a thief—there's a thief."

The headmaster of the school heard this noise and came outside of the school building to see what was up. Now the old man didn't want to be disgraced in public and especially in front of all of those children. So he told the headmaster, "Please come near and use an old man's eye and look into this bag to know if there is a rooster or not."

So the headmaster approached and with an elderly eye looked into the bag, and then drove the children away and said that there was no rooster there. Then the headmaster called the old man inside of his room and settled with him, and warned him severely about stealing and gave him a few coins to buy food. The old man thanked him, took out the rooster and gave it to the headmaster, who turned it loose behind the school.

The first time I heard this story, it was used as an illustration in the middle of a sermon given by a Togolese preach-

## 6. "Old Man's Eye."

er. Some of the Europeans in the audience were incensed, and after the service showed great righteous indignation by talking amongst themselves about how unscriptural such a story was: "How typical it is of the African, who knows no truth and distorts the law of God!"

The problem with those Europeans was they didn't know much about Ewe custom. If the old man had been shamed by all of the children, he would have committed suicide before sundown! In settling the matter privately, no harm was done. In Africa, if you are a wise person (elderly), you don't permit your mouth to say everything your eyes can see! To a West African, the *spirit* of the law should take priority over the *letter*. It is still this issue that a part of the western church never has known how to handle. Dilemmas become ordeals. And still a portion of the church would stone the woman taken in adultery—just as surely as the Pharisees interpreting the law of Moses. But Jesus saw a wiser option. He looked in the sack and chased the children away, too. No one should believe that he condoned the actions of this unfortunate woman, but he saved her just as surely as the schoolmaster saved the old man.

Many times a beautiful seashell picked up at the ocean shore will have delicate colorings and a beautiful formation, but will be encrusted with barnacle-like organisms that mar the shell's beauty. One of the appropriate ways of removing this encrustation is with a weak solution of hydrochloric acid and water. Slowly the solution is applied to the offending barnacles with a brush. If one has much patience and a considerable amount of time, the goal can be reached. Another way of removing the encrustation is to dunk the shell in pure hydrochloric acid. The barnacles will go bubbling away—but, of course, the shell is also destroyed. Is it any wonder that multitudes of people have been so turned off by the church's concept of justice that they have been forever alienated from the church's declared mission of being Christ's ambassador of love, understanding, and forgiveness?

Christ has called us to a ministry of healing, and he would lead us away from harsh preaching and dogmatic witnessing. Clerics and laymen must absolutely *relearn* the basic biblical dicta that the law always accuses and kills, while only the gospel heals and gives life. Until we begin to believe this, our communication will be bad news instead of good news. As a witness for the Master, I must not forget that exhortation is not a substitute for healing! Yes, there is a time to throw stones and identify the rooster in the bag (even Africans know that for habitual criminals, swift judgment is the only remedy). But I have decided that I am going to come to that action very slowly. A steady diet of Christian exhortation will destroy my hearers just as quickly as if the message were from the book of Numbers.

I will not lose my balance or spiritual perception by neglecting the sure announcements of the judgment of God and that the wages of sin are death—and yet, let me come down on the side of healing and understanding. Let me look in the bag with an old man's eye more often than I have done in the past.

## Christ the Fisherman

The names of God, as found primarily in the Old Testament, make a beautiful study in any language and culture. West Africans find special significance in the names of God because of the great importance that their cultures place on names (see chapter 6).

Africa is still part of the older culture. Its people feel that a person's name *should* have significant meaning and should match the strong characteristics of his personality. For many Africans, God's names represent attributes of his very power. Isaiah's description of the Messiah with such words as Emmanuel, Counselor, Prince of Peace, etc. is a wondrous thing in the minds of Christians of the two-thirds world.

The reader might well imagine that a good percentage of West Africans are still very adept at hunting and fishing for their livelihood. When they hear preachers and teachers from the west talk about the many names for Christ (Son of God, Son of Man, Messiah, Savior, Shepherd), they are surprised that they have never heard us refer to him as the Great Fisherman! I remember one old Mossi pastor who had never been to school, but had become literate in his own language to be able to read the scriptures. He went through the New Testament and with amazing insight pointed out all the places in the gospels where Jesus said something about fishing, taught someone else what he knew about fishing, or was handling or eating fish himself. This pastor then gave the following exposition of Luke 9:57-62:

Jesus was a great fisherman. We know that because he knew that you have to use different kinds of bait for different fish. He invites us all to be fishers of men. People, too, are very different and need different kinds of bait. These six verses show us that Jesus found three different kinds of fish and used three different kinds of bait from his fishing basket (tackle box). Jesus knew about the flexibility and wisdom that a good fisher (like a good witness) must have. Here are the three fish:

1. MR. FEET BEFORE HIS HEAD (someone who talks before he thinks):
This man came to Jesus and said to him, "Lord, I will follow you wherever you go." The Master reminded him that even foxes and birds have homes and nests, but that the Son of Man doesn't have a permanent address. This man was impetuous and seemingly willing to follow Christ at a moment's

notice. When Christ saw this fish, he reached back in his basket and pulled out some bait that was just right. He was admonishing this fish, "Can you count the cost? You want to follow me very quickly, but do you know the price of living my kind of life?" Let's now look at Fish #2.

2. MR. HEAVY FEET (hesitant to make a decision): When Jesus confronted this fish, the fish did not speak first. In fact, the Lord said to him, "Follow me." But he answered, "Lord, let me first go and bury my father." Of course, the man's father was not yet dead. We Africans know that what he was really saying was that he wasn't ready yet to follow the Lord. He wanted to wait until his father *was* dead and he would inherit his father's wealth, and then he would be in a stable position to be able to follow the Lord. When Jesus reached back and got the bait for this kind of fish, it was an entirely different variety than for "Mr. Feet Before His Head." The bait Jesus offered this fish was to "let the dead bury their dead." Let the ideas from the secular world take care of their own problems. You need to abandon that thing and be ready to preach the kingdom of God. Now do you notice how different the bait is between Fish #1 and Fish #2? Let's look at #3.

3. MR. DRUM WITH TWO HEADS (someone who talks out of both sides of his mouth): This fish spoke up for himself and said, "Lord, I will follow you, but let me first go bid them farewell, who are at my house." This seems like a reasonable demand, but when we see Christ's answer to him, we know that the Lord saw a very bad flaw in this man's character that made him unfit for discipleship. Why the European missionary has never told us that Jesus was indeed a wise fisherman, I don't

**7. "Lunga" Two-headed Drum.**

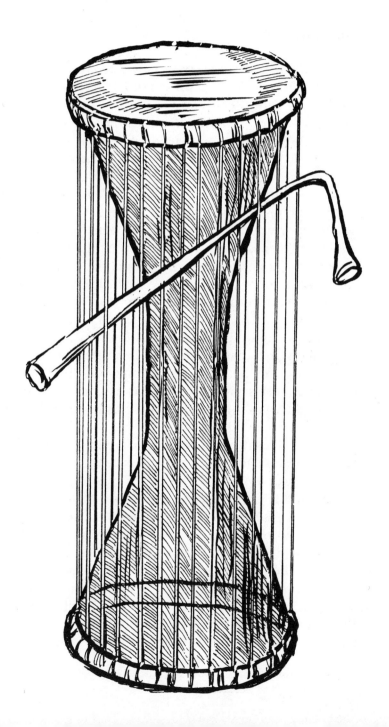

know. Maybe it was because he doesn't know fish the way we do!

In Luke, the fifth chapter, Jesus taught Simon Peter quite a lesson in fishing methods. We see that Peter was not paying attention while Jesus was talking to the crowd; so maybe to get Peter's attention and also to get away from the crowd, he stepped into Peter's boat. He asked him to put out a little from shore. Peter naturally had to keep the boat in position so that it would not get too far away from the land and Christ's voice not be heard. Possibly to thank Peter after the end of the sermon, he instructed him to go out into deeper water and throw out his nets for some fish. We can hear Peter saying, "Now, Lord, you might be a good lecturer, but you don't know anything about fishing. One can only fish here at night, and we have already fished all night and caught nothing. There is no way to catch anything this time of day." Nevertheless, when Peter did finally obey, he got quite a lesson in fishing methods! There were so many fish that he couldn't haul them in himself and had to call for his partners to come and help. In the 10th verse of that segment, Peter was astonished at what had taken place and Jesus said, "Do not be afraid. From now on you will catch men."

Peter learned his fishing lesson quite well. In the book of Acts we see that he threw his net and caught 3,000 men on the day of Pentecost.

Most West African languages have more than one word for our word *fisherman*. They generally use different words, depending on the method of fishing: by net, by trap, or those who catch fish by spearing. Maybe the very structure of their language helps the African to see how skillful Jesus really was—relating to both fish and people. I think it is refreshing that the Mossi can see all the great attributes of Christ that we see, and can even add a few more. One of them is Christ the Fisherman.

## To Know But Not Show

In the previous pages "Christ the Fisherman," we looked at the insight an African preacher had on the passage of scripture in Luke, the ninth chapter. From that African's knowledge of fishing methods, he drew parallels to Christ's methods of reaching for individuals. There is a verse in that passage that we from the west find very difficult. The trouble is, we don't understand the figures of speech of the middle east and the Orient relative to death and inheritance, nor do we find it easy to interpret indirect and enigmatic phrases for which the literal translation is quite meaningless. Westerners generally have difficulty with understanding the *second* agenda of a particular message, because our culture tends to consistently "say what we mean and mean what we say." The verses I am interested in exploring are verses 59 and 60:

He said to another man, "Follow me." But the man replied, "Lord, first let me go and bury my father." Jesus said to him, "Let the dead bury their own dead, but you go and proclaim the kingdom of God."

Matthew's account of this same dialogue tells us that this man was a disciple. Now, I don't take this to mean that he was one of *the* disciples. For at this time in Christ's ministry, quite a large number of people were following him and were called disciples. The presence of many *potential* disciples was probably one of the reasons why the Lord chose this time to teach an indispensable principle relating to the cost of *true* discipleship.

Two things are very important for our understanding. First—in verse 59, when the man asked for the Lord's permission to bury his father, we should not take it to mean that the man's father was actually dead. This is a common expression in the Orient, Africa, and the Middle East relating to inheritance through the kinship system of family social structure. "Let me bury my father" means "Let me keep doing what I am doing until that time when my social status will be changed by the death of my father. The ensuing social and economic stability will then allow me to change my lifestyle or to take on new responsibilities." The second thing we need to know is that the actual words of Christ in verse 60 should not be taken literally either! "Let the dead bury their own dead" certainly does not refer to the actual interment of a corpse. I submit that it refers to an ordering of priorities—the higher values of the *kingdom* in relation to earthly values such as inheritance and personal social gain.

The following story will illustrate what I believe Christ intended to teach this potential disciple. The story also shows us one of the characteristics of leadership that many African societies strongly value: coping in the face of obvious peril. Note that in the story, Death is personified as someone who can communicate with ordinary living people.

Death was selling a cow. Thus, when one man bought the cow, the townspeople and the town chief quarreled with him and told him not to buy it. They said, "Don't you know that you will die?"

The man answered, "Yes, I know, but I am still going to buy it." Death told him that he would give him three years to live; that he didn't want any money, but that at the end of three years he would come and take him. The man thus agreed to the bargain. He paid nothing for the cow. Death had told him that to collect for the debt, he would cause him to die by a stomach ailment or a head ailment, which the man had agreed to. His family was very sorrowful, and his mother and father cried. He told them not to worry.

Now when the three years were up, Death came and said, "I'll give you three more years." When these

8. Death.

three years finished, Death again came back; but the man was still not startled and he didn't react at all. He greeted Death and said, "Well, I see you've come." And Death said that it was true, that he had come; but that he was ready to give him two more years.

When these latest two years were up, Death returned and said, "It's true. This time I have come definitely." The man who bargained for the cow acknowledged his arrival and said that Death should note that he was still alive. After greeting Death, he said that he was going to go home. Death gave him permission to do so and said that he should go home, and that they should meet again tomorrow.

The next day when Death came back and found the man, he noticed that the man was back in the field cultivating where he had seen him the day before, and that his cultivating had progressed very well since then. When he saw this he said, "I am going to release you. If you were the responsible person (the chief) of a village, you would handle the situation well. You can risk the unexpected, so I am releasing you from our bargain."

In the six West African societies in which we have lived, they all give high rewards for the individual who can have knowledge of a certain danger or risk and then ignore the obvious by not reacting. To *know* but not *show* is a highly desirable human characteristic. This is the quality that "Death" rewarded in the individual who bought the cow from him. This is why he said, "You are able to rule a village. If an unexpected circumstance comes—you can face that difficulty with dignity and trust." The key to the story is the self-confidence possessed by the man when he could work in the field and make a visible showing in spite of the fact that Death was looking over his shoulder and was ready to take him. There is a similar message of Christ to the potential disciple. "If you can forget about this world's system," Christ was saying, "and let those who count on this world's system bury your father, then you can be my disciple. You'll be fit to go and preach the kingdom if you can raise your eyes with confidence and faith to higher priorities. These priorities supersede the normal, legitimate inheritance system that your culture has taught you."

As in the story of Death and the cow, no one would deny that death is a disaster and ever-present. By ignoring the obvious the man in that story illustrates exactly what Christ would teach all of us about the risk we must be willing to take to do his bidding. A valuable disciple in his kingdom must be willing to "lose his life so he can find it" (see Mark 8:35, Matthew 16:25). There is that paradox again! We would like to take the risk out of serving Christ. We would like to hold on to this world's system and "bury our fathers" and still serve him. He insists that we be willing to forfeit the natural rules of security and "buy Death's cow" as an act of faith. Christ rewards those who can *know* and not *show*.

## Mane Suşri
## (Make a Covering)

Jesus, talking about forgiveness and tolerance, gives the illustration of a servant who owed a great sum of money (many thousands and thousands of dollars). The debtor pleaded with the householder (patron) for mercy. He was forgiven the complete debt! Subsequent to this magnanimous reprieve, the servant turned around and refused to forgive a very small, insignificant sum. That is where we pick up the story in verse 32 of Matthew 18:

Then the master called the servant in. "You wicked servant," he said, "I canceled all that debt of yours because you begged me to. Shouldn't you have had mercy on your fellow servant just as I had on you?" In anger his master turned him over to the jailers to be tortured, until he should pay back all he owed. This is how my heavenly Father will treat each of you unless you forgive your brother from your heart.

In one of the African languages that I have come to love (Mori), the word for "forgive" is a very lovely concept (an idea). It is related to a hat. You have to know something about the West African sun in countries on the great savannah near the Sahara Desert to really appreciate the value of a conical hat. It's called a "zugu sugri" (head roof). The second word (sugri) for this hat is the same as is used for the covering of a house, or what we all know as a typical African hut.

A hat is a "head covering." A roof is a "house covering." They look very much alike. The expression to mean *forgiveness* (mane sugri) is "make a covering."

"Make a covering and give to me," says the repentant person. If you agree to that, you'll say to him, "I'll make a covering for you." And Jesus said, "So likewise shall my heavenly Father do also unto you..."

Tolerance, forgiveness, long-suffering—the simple fruits of the Spirit—are included in "making a covering." The ministry of this covering of forgiveness is really the opposite from the attitude of criticism and exposure. I recently heard a story from a good friend of mine about the artist/painter of Alexander the Great. He not only was a great artist, but loved and revered this young genius general. All artists know that every person has a best angle. But when this artist would put Alexander the Great in that position, an ugly battle scar would show up on his cheek. He said, "I don't want to paint the scar, and yet that's the best angle." So he would turn him to another angle, but he would always come back to the one "best" position. But the scar would show. He didn't want to be hypocritical and not put in the scar,

9. Hat.

because then people would say, "But Alexander has a scar there!" So he ended up painting him from his chosen position, but with his hand to his cheek in a relaxed, contemplative mood, with a finger covering the scar.

The scriptures teach us to depict our brother or sister—from the best position and with "mane sugri" (with a little covering in certain places). God helps us to show our brothers and sisters in their best light, instead of saying, "God, look! Shame, shame—God, did you see that?" Shouldn't we cry: "O Lord, cover my brother. I cover him. I forgive him. I love him. O God, don't look at that little blemish."

Would you agree with me that when Jesus gave the keys of the kingdom to the disciples and said, "What you bind, I'll bind. What you loose, I'll loose" (see Matthew 16:19; 18:18), this is related to this element? Let us not go to the "heathen" across the sea—or our neighbor across the street—and say, "God forgives you," and we ourselves do the work of the gospel from an isolation booth. I don't really think you can be a "sent one" until you become so involved with the culture, a congregation, a family, that you have something to *forgive them for*. How can they believe the forgiveness of God until they see our willingness to model this grace?

Why shouldn't we ask the Lord to help us *find* something about which to forgive our brother/sister? Wouldn't that be a shocker? Who says that forgiveness need only be a *reaction*! Why not set out in the morning *seeking* to administer forgiveness as an active intent of the spirit? Can you imagine how traffic patterns and driving skills would be affected!

The paradox of the scriptures includes how to forgive through service. Christ gave us the example of this type of covering when he grabbed the towel. He did the job of a servant. It is amazing what you can cover with service.

Do we want to shield some of the harsh rays of interpersonal interaction? Let's grab a towel. Mane sugri—make a covering.

## Mane Sugri (Part II)

Dilemma: How to "cover" (shield) someone's sin so repentance and healing can be affected through proper timing? We have great trouble with this in the west. We like things "up front" and coming to the "bottom line"— quickly and to the point! How can *love* cover *sins*?

One of the best examples this writer has learned from Africa that relates to the aspect of forgiveness (make a covering) is the following story, translated directly from the Mossi vernacular.

There was a chief that had a kingdom, and he was a very worthy person and liked all of his subjects. Now, all of his subjects loved him also. If difficulty came to his people, he really helped them well. All the time he was behind his people and did them well, and the people's hearts were agreeable toward him. If they needed land, he helped them find land to farm; if a man needed a wife, the chief would help him. When there was trouble between husband and wives, the chief took a personal interest in these cases, and often settled them to the satisfaction of both parties. However, the chief had one fault.

When someone died in the village and they buried him, the chief would steal out in the middle of the night and go to uncover the dead one and cut off certain body parts to make medicine.[1] When the people came to understand that it was their chief that was robbing the graves at night and subsequently hid these things until he could sell them, their hearts were fearful, because one does not tell an African chief directly that he is the one who is doing something wrong. So, the chief continued doing this month after month.

One man came and said that he was going to find the answer to this problem. The next time someone died in the village and they buried him, the man climbed a tree just before dark near the grave. Sure enough, the chief came during the night with a short-handled hoe over his shoulder with which to dig. "Kours, Kours, Kours" went the hoe. (The man sitting in the tree was watching.) When the hidden spectator saw what the chief was doing, he took his own hoe handle and hit the tree, "Ko, Ko, Ko." The chief quickly stopped and stood up (the chief never let anyone accompany him). And the chief said to himself, "Yoa! Where did the noise come from?" He stopped and hunched down and listened and listened and waited and thought he might see someone. He saw no one and did not know from where the noise had come. He thought perhaps it was not a person; maybe it was something else that did it.

So, he began to dig again—"Kours, Kours, Kours." So, the man in the tree tapped again, "Ko, Ko, Ko." The chief quickly stooped down and looked and looked and looked. This time he waited longer than before, but he didn't see anybody. He didn't know where the noise came from—he didn't know it was a person doing it. He thought: "Perhaps it was not a person who did it; perhaps it was only an animal." He began to dig the third time and the person in the tree tapped again, "Ko, Ko, Ko." Now the chief came to think, "I know it is not a thing, but it is a person." So he covered up the grave with the hoe and went home.

Early the next morning the chief's drum beat called the whole village to his place. Everyone came. As all of the villagers were coming, they kept asking each

**10. Grave Scene.**

other: "What do you suppose the chief is calling us together for?" When they had all gathered, the chief stood up and he said that something had happened to him in the bush that he did not like, and he wanted to tell everyone so they would understand. "Something went, 'Ko, Ko, Ko' at me in the bush. Whatever it is that would tap, 'Ko, Ko, Ko,' I don't want this thing to tap at me again!"

No one knew what this thing could be. The villagers talked amongst themselves as to what the chief meant. "What is it that taps, 'Ko, Ko, Ko,' like that so that the chief was displeased? Why would the chief say that he doesn't like to hear 'Ko, Ko, Ko'?"

But the person who was tapping knew, and he finally stood and said, "It's true—it's true what the chief said and it is good. When the chief is out in the bush, it is not good that 'Ko, Ko' taps at him so that he doesn't like it. But there is one thing that must be considered—it is the 'Kours, Kours' that makes the 'Ko, Ko' tap. If the 'Kours, Kours' doesn't go 'Kours, Kours,' perhaps the 'Ko, Ko' won't tap again!"

He himself knew and the chief knew, but everybody else sat in silence. Nobody else was involved. So the chief left off grave robbing. He knew that if he kept robbing the graves, this fact would become known and he would be shamed.

The chief was a good chief, and his function as the leader of his community was well appreciated—even by the individual who wanted to cure him of his bad habit. Now, it is because the citizen loved the chief that he was willing to "cover" his deed and "expose" it at the same time.

Forgiveness as seen by the Mossi is not covering over and obscuring a fault. But it is a delicate *balance* of exposing the fault in the mind of the guilty party (by the administrator of forgiveness), yet not destroying him with the naked glare of the full light of revelation.

It would be a mistake to think that the one administering forgiveness wants to hide the fault or conceal the wrongdoing completely. Rather, it is a shielding of the sun's intensity by the hat, or covering the glaring ugly scar like the artist. Or, in this case, it was the shielding of the chief from the unbearable public shame that his society would heap on him in judgment if all was revealed instantly (he would have committed suicide).

And above all things have fervent love among yourselves, for love will cover a multitude of sins (see 1 Peter 4:8).

Why do so many in the church act like clumsy butchers (destroying the patient) instead of saving the patient like a skillful surgeon? Brothers and sisters of the west—let us continue to learn this eastern book!

### Note

1. The reader must understand that in an animistic society, life force and the belief in the supernatural are often equated with objects. Power is thought to be resident in certain objects. Some of these objects are body parts of humans and animals. Special roots and herbs are valued for their power of healing as well as power of protection. Thus, the chief could sell the body parts for a high price to the shaman, who would grind them and bag them into little pouches carried by those seeking special powers or protection.

# 3

# Cultural Filters Inhibit Clear Perception

Caution! The title and content of this chapter are not intended to insult westerners or put them on the defensive. The reader should not confuse the *part* for the *whole* or vice versa. My willingness to assert that *some* aspects of North American culture/society prohibit clear understanding of scripture should not be understood to imply that *all* western culture is defective *or* that no elements of our heritage are beneficial to aid spiritual cognition. It is a commentary on God's patience and grace that he can still use imperfect instruments to build his kingdom. It was so with the first apostles. In spite of many ethnocentric and slanted interpretations of scripture in evangelistic efforts, how wonderfully God has used the economy, the commitment, the dedication of westerners to take the glorious message of the kingdom of Christ around the world. The unprecedented numbers of these people and their effectiveness cannot be denied. In fact the secular world refuses to recognize the enormous impact of Christian missions on the world's philosophies. Christianity, as carried by its ambassadors (and in spite of their faults), has changed the ideological face of the globe. Yet, ironically, it is the success of Christian missions that remains one of the strongest arguments of why we westerners resist any notion that we might need to learn something new. It's the ethic of capitalism that says "what works must be good" and "you can't knock success" or "if it ain't broke, don't fix it."

I am a product of the west and would not try to deny that. Nonetheless, Africans and Asians have taught me that I need to be always learning to become a better communicator. These brothers and sisters instruct me in many things which my culture overlooks or where it possesses cultural insensitivity. Many of these blind spots are excusable because their cause is a simple lack of information. For instance, how could someone from the west know that for many of Africa's people certain scriptural passages in the gospels and in Revelation need to be translated or interpreted differently in English? I specifically speak of the passages that refer to Jesus who "stands at the door and *knocks*." For some tribes anyone who knocks is a thief. Robbers knock to determine if anyone is at home! If no one stirs, the thief then has courage to come in and steal. The Revelation passage also includes Jesus saying, "If anyone hears my voice." This is the key: Any acquaintance's voice is readily recognized and so the person seeking entry would always be identified by the tone of the voice and not by knocking. A thief would never use the voice so as not to be identified. Here a contextualized translation would have Jesus saying, "I stand at the door and *call*."

All six of the segments in this chapter raise the issue of western culture as a barrier to a better understanding of scripture. These statements are not meant to cause offense but to focus the attention of the reader on the intention of the author. Our wonderful culture has, nonetheless, prohibited us from understanding the words of Jesus about *"Making Friends With Mammon."* Also, our concept of equality as found in the U.S. Constitution doesn't allow us to see that God actually favors *inequality* in many contexts. Or how can our culture allow us to understand that the fifth commandment, "Honor your father and your mother," is really *Not For Little Kids* as much as it is for adults. In this chapter we will also look at the eagle, *A Look at the Birds*, the American symbol of greatness and how differently other cultures may see that symbol. And in *Olungawema* we'll look at a story we tell our children which the Eve and Fon also tell. It reveals a lot about them and us.

## Making Friends with Mammon

The scriptures and West Africans both have a philosophy about being shrewd with business dealings. These concepts are not easy for us. Most North American evangelicals would like their world to be divided up into neat categories, where there is no ambiguity about what is right and what is wrong; what is good and what is bad; what is white and what is black; what is holy and what is sinful. If we had our druthers, we would wish that all decisions could be easily handled—completely in one category or another. This characteristic, especially of the religious world in North American life, is called "two-valued orientation" (North Americans aren't the only ones with this predisposition).

We have difficulty with the shades of meaning and the combination of meaning, just as we have difficulty with the word "compromise." In contrast to this tendency, I have found that Europeans see the word "compromise" as being a very positive attribute, working out and working through a process of accommodations so that all can be happy. "Compromise" in American English, however, generally has negative connotations. This stems from our unwillingness to consider that something might best be categorized as being partly in two compartments rather than totally, absolutely, cleanly, and neatly being put in either one or the other.

It is not my intention here to imply that a two-valued orientation is always wrong or always inferior. There are indeed instances when one must make an absolute choice for the sake of deep principles and values where some of the absolutes that God makes very clear to us are concerned. However, to take that premise and then project a system whereby all information and all ideas must be processed *only* through a rigid grid of "either/or" is to deny that truth is more of a *process*—dynamic not static—than a totally finished *product* around which you can draw a definitive line of exclusivity.

For instance, few elements of my American culture give me a background to correctly understand Christ's parable, in Luke 16, of the shrewd manager. Jesus told his disciples about a rich man whose manager was accused of wasting his possessions. You will remember that this manager considered his alternatives under the accusation and ultimately pleased his boss. He used mammon (wheat and olive oil, representing collateral in wealth) to both enrich his master's coffers by liquidating bad debts, and at the same time make friends with the debtors so that even if he would finally lose his job, he would have a place to light.

Verse eight of that chapter says:

> The master commended the dishonest manager because he had acted shrewdly. For the people of this world are more shrewd in dealing with their own kind than are the people of the light. I tell you, use worldly wealth to gain friends for yourselves, so that when it is gone, you will be welcomed into eternal dwellings.

I believe this is one of the things that Christ was telling the rich young ruler in Matthew 19. Not only was he to divest himself of his present security system and have a change of heart so that he could trust and rely on God, but in the process he was to make friends with mammon. West African Christians don't have nearly the trouble interpreting how Christ could encourage someone to be shrewd as do people in the west influenced by the Protestant ethic. Please note I would not suggest that one system is better than another, but simply that one system makes for less dissonance in interpreting what Christ might have meant. Consider the following African parable to illustrate this thought:

> I heard of an African chief who had about 20 wives; and when he would be with each one separately (talking about conjugal rights), he would give each one a waist belt[1] and he'd say, "You—I love you more than all the others—then be careful and don't let the other wives come to know that you have this belt. And don't talk, either." Now, when all the wives are in the field working, and when the chief comes near to watch the wives and the children hoeing, he'd say, "Yes, I love all of my wives, but the one with the money belt I love the most."

The meaning is, of course, very obvious. One wife's name would be Sibedu, and another Kwilega, and another Goma. But if he called one's name and said, "I love all of my wives, but Goma I love the most," the others would know whom he preferred. But by talking ambiguously and giving each one this money belt secretly, he made each one think, "Ah, I'm the preferred one!" So she'd work harder than her strength would normally allow to please him for his selection of her.

This is a very funny story to West Africans because it gives them great pleasure to know of a shrewd person who is able to manipulate people and personal wealth to their own gain without actually causing injury to someone else.

The nub of this whole matter, however, is the *motive* behind his shrewd manipulation.

Savannah people believe that Christ expects his disciples to be able to "work the system" in whatever context or culture they find themselves. The key, however, to "working the system" is that it not be done for unethical personal or selfish gain. Emphasis in this issue should be placed upon the word *neglect*. If one can't make friends with mammon, then one is neglecting to utilize a tool with which he should be competent. The emphasis is not that one become shrewd for selfish reasons, but rather shrewd so as not to neglect being able to maximize the system at one's disposal.

The African chief with the 20 wives is lauded, not because he can get so much more work out of 20 women, each thinking she is the preferred; but rather because by using a money belt, he has increased the self-esteem of each woman—the by-product of which (only naturally) is an increased productivity. This, then, is the "making friends with mammon" that the African sees so clearly and which his American counterpart has great difficulty seeing through the present cultural filters of our concept of truth and ethics.

I believe this is substantiated by the closing verses of the parable in Luke 16:

> Whoever can be trusted with very little can also be trusted with much, and whoever is dishonest with very little will also be dishonest with much. So if you have not been trustworthy in handling worldly wealth, who will trust you with true riches? (vv 10-11).

Christ, subsequently, really zeros in on the Pharisees, whose love for money was causing them to use it (the system) in a way that was detestable in God's sight.

If my culture teaches me to think in a two-valued orientation so that I put all meanings for the word "shrewd" in the negative basket, then there's no way that I can understand how Christ could actually encourage a form of shrewdness in order to make friends with mammon.

## Inequality in God's Measure

So the last shall be first, and the first last: for many be called, but few chosen (Matthew 20:16).

Shocking words, these! Christ uses this expression overtly a number of times in his teaching and implies it in still other passages. The idea seems incompatible with fair play and social ethics in achievement-oriented western society. How unthinkable that Christ should tell us that he's going to flip over or *reverse* the very sequence and ranking order we clamor for! The last first and the first last!

This saying both precedes and follows the story of the householder who hired laborers in his field (Matthew 20). An amazing thing occurred at the end of the day in this story, for the householder paid the laborers some very strange wages! It was very undemocratic behavior. In fact, his action would certainly call for a strike by union members if it happened to them on the North American work scene.

What seems to be inequality and unfairness from our world view and perspective is not nearly as difficult to understand from the viewpoint of African savannah people. They live in a social system we would describe as "inequality." Traditional African society (like that of the Old Testament) will purposely "*advantage*" one son (usually the oldest), giving him economic authority over his brothers and sisters upon the death or disability of the family head. With this advantage, however, comes great responsibility. You will agree that this is quite unthinkable in modern North American society.

Life is full of inequality on the savannah, where someone with special talent is rewarded without much jealousy. No attempt is made to treat everyone alike. Differences of abilities and strengths are seen as the normal plan of God's creation. And people accept being disadvantaged or left out with much more grace in African society than one sees in the west.

Even Europeans point out a disadvantage of America's "equality" kick as mirrored in our educational system. They say the American grade school, junior high, and high school systems are so intent on treating everyone equally that the highs and lows of human achievement tend to be lopped off. Outstanding students are held back from reaching their potential; and slow students who *should* be encouraged to follow a stream of vocational training are pulled along, in the name of equality, by a system designed to end up in college. The latter are usually thus turned off by the whole educational picture and also jeopardized in their chances to build self-esteem and future fulfillment as adults. This unfortunate system is perpetrated in the name of equality.

Most of Africa refuses to play this foolish game, because they recognize that people *are* unequal and that inequality is both valid and desirable. Inequality, in Africa, is often directly related to human behavior, which the African believes merits unequal recompense and treatment. Consider the following story of three unequal wives who were rewarded on the basis of performance and attitudes.

There was a man who had three wives. Among these three wives one did well and was considered his favorite. One did very well, and another did only adequately, but the last didn't do well even a little bit. This man liked to treat his wives in a good manner and he was kind and generous. One day it happened that all three wives' mothers came and met each other and came to his home to visit their daughters, each mother coming from her own home but meeting at the same time at their daughters' husband's home. They visited their daughters for a while, and then the day came when they all decided that they would leave together.

Now, the husband had prepared a gift for each mother-in-law, all wrapped up, that she would carry away with her, as was the tradition. For his favorite wife he had killed and prepared a sheep and rice and a gift of $20, all wrapped up in a bundle which she carried away on her head as she left. For the second wife he killed a chicken and had added rice and $10 in her bundle. For the third wife he killed a guinea fowl and had added rice and a gift of $4.

The morning of their departure, the husband stood at the gate as each mother-in-law and her daughter came by to receive their gift. According to custom, the daughter carries the gift and walks beside her own mother down the road a few kilometers to help her at the beginning of her long journey of walking home. The girls then say good-bye to their mother down the road, and on their way back to the husband's house, stop off in the bush to cut and carry firewood for their own cooking needs. So this is exactly what they did.

The mothers then went on ahead carrying their own loads. After they had gone down the road for a ways, they stopped to rest their loads and they said to each other, "Let's untie our bundles and see what we've received as gifts." Now, when they had set their loads down, they soon discovered that one had received a whole sheep and $20, another only a chicken and

$10, and the third a guinea hen and only $4. The three discussed the matter.

Those receiving the guinea hen and the chicken said, "No way—let's return and ask him. We gave birth with blood to give him a wife, we didn't give birth with water. And it's not right to do like this and give one a whole sheep and only give us a chicken and a guinea hen." They began to fight with each other and walk back to ask the husband of their daughters. When they reached him they asked, "We came to ask you why it is that one got a sheep and more money, and one got a chicken and less money, and one got a guinea hen and even less money. We don't understand the meaning of this, and we gave hard birth so that you could have a wife. You shouldn't have done this to us."

So the husband told them, "Don't talk. Everyone go into her own child's house. Sit and rest for a little while. Your daughters will return; they're out getting firewood. And when they come back, just sit and listen."

The husband waited at the gate. With him he had taken some grain and a calabash of water and stood waiting for them. The first one to come back was the one who had received the guinea hen and the least amount of money. As she came up to the gate, he got up and met her. Before she threw down her wood he said, "Ah, good, take my grain and grind it and make me some flour water,[2] because from the time that you left I have eaten nothing."

The guinea hen mother's daughter answered, "Get lost—have you lost your mind—I've got work, and I've come back and haven't even rested—go away, your senses have left you." And he took the grain back and

**11. Women's Work.**

waited for the daughter of the one who had received the chicken.

When she came he said, "Ah, good! Take this grain and make me some grain water, because I'm hungry."

She answered, "Wait until I've lowered the wood and rest a while, then I'll do it. I haven't even unloaded— and you're asking me to run and get you water. Wait until I've rested and I'll fix it for you."

So he stayed sitting at the gate waiting for his third wife. When she arrived he got up and said, "Good! Take my grain and grind it and make some flour water, because since you've left I've tasted nothing."

And she answered, "Oh, that's all right." And she threw down her wood on the spot and took the grain to the grinding table, ground the grain between two stones, made him his flour water, and brought it to her husband to drink.

Thus each mother sitting in her own child's house heard her child's words, and they had no more questions for the man. They all got up and left together without a word.

What an advantage the African world view gives for understanding the story that Jesus told his disciples in Matthew 20! The wages that the householder paid in the scriptural story caused those who had been working a long time to grumble. But Jesus told the story in answer to the disciples' question in the previous chapter, "We who have left all and followed you, what are we going to get out of it?" (see Matthew 19:27). Jesus wanted to show the disciples that those who are expecting to be *first* based on this world's system of evaluation and measurement of fair play are actually going to be last; and those who are willing to work for him with integrity, not worrying nearly as much about recompense but working from love, are like the wife who so loved her husband that she was willing to comply with a seemingly unreasonable demand to please him.

## Not for Little Kids

It has been our family's privilege to interact with indigenous church organizations in 14 west and central African nations over a 30 year period. We've made an amazing discovery! Africans don't believe the fifth commandment is for kids. I think they're right.

> Honor your father and mother, so that you may live long in the land the Lord your God is giving you (Exodus 20:12).

I heard it when I was in Sunday school. I heard it when I was a teenager in church, but I don't hear it anymore now that I am an adult. What a shame! For it is now, when I have children of my own, that I need most to honor my father and mother.

Many African proverbs can illustrate the significance of this thought. Here is one that is very poignant:

> If you see a young man carrying his father on his back—thank the old man (father).

What are the implications of this proverb?

DO YOUR PARENTS A FAVOR—HONOR THEM

Even if you don't like them, respect your parents' personal merits or demerits. The scriptures say to honor them. Traditional kinship cultures know that this pays, now and forever. Most Africans try to honor their parents by obey-

ing their commands in all things lawful. They try to antici-
pate the wishes of their parents, and they also are on guard
to spare their parents from vexation. As a rule, in all societies parents have more love for children than children
have for their parents. Parents tend to make greater sacrifices on their children's behalf. Sometimes this is neither
appreciated nor reciprocated.

Since we are seldom better than our parents, it should
not be difficult to honor them. Traditional kinship societies
find great social stability from the inequality of parents having a certain authority all their lives. What an undemocratic thought! Kinship peoples around the world never see
themselves equal to their parents. Modern society has
strayed from the scriptural pattern.[3]

DO YOURSELF A FAVOR—HONOR YOUR PARENTS

Ptah-Hotep, an Egyptian author of Abraham's time, said
this: "The son who accepts the words of his father will
grow old in consequence of so doing." This part is the clear
guarantee of the fifth commandment, the first commandment with promise. One should be able to expect the blessing of God because of obedience in honoring parents; but
the key ingredient that pays such high dividends is the
word *submission*. If an individual has a mind-set of submis-
siveness because he or she continually practices "prefer-
ring one another," that person is going to reap the social
dividends that will allow long life. The Dagomba (of
Ghana), for example, know that honoring your biological
superiors *transfers* to other God-ordained natural laws that
any society needs to be able to dwell (live long)—both individually in the community and collectively in the immediate social environment.

Now here's the key to why this is not for kids: *When I,
an adult, ignore or dishonor my parent's position of
headship, I remove myself from the dependent role of a
child and the submission that this necessitates.* Kinship
societies are sure that God knew when this law was given

that the individual who will not submit to parents will have great difficulty in submitting to other authorities needed for stability in any community.

DO YOUR CHILDREN A FAVOR—HONOR YOUR PARENTS

The reason the African proverb says that you should thank the old man who is getting a free ride on the back of his robust son is obvious (to the African). One does not teach others (by words) to honor. This lesson is better *caught* than *taught*. The old man is getting a ride in his infirmity because *he* was a model to his son by honoring his own parents. In turn, his son just naturally will honor his father by helping him when he is crippled and weak. Where do my children learn to honor me? They'll honor me when *they see me honor my elders*.   .

What a devastating thing we are doing in modern society! There are hardly any three-generation families to be found. The biblical model is that the grandparents *and* the parents all help to raise the children. The children benefit from the wisdom of another generation, which is blended with the ideas and methods of their immediate parents, to give a broader, wider perspective on the philosophy of life and social and religious values. One need not take time here to point out the emotional and spiritual deprivation that modern society is fostering by the breakdown of traditional biblical family structures.

CONTRASTING TWO WORLDS

Let's briefly look at the shocking differences between a world dominated by contract, individualism, and independence, and a world dominated by kinship with reciprocal interrelated ties in a sense of communal unity.

In the contract-dominated world, a child is taught independence and individualism at an early age. "When you grow up, Johnny/Mary, you will be and do thus and such—all by yourself. Mommy and Daddy will not be there to help you." When the child is born, very few family members are near enough to touch; in fact, Mom is often still anes-thetized. We immediately isolate the child behind glass while relatives who are there peek and gawk from a dis-tance (in the name of hygiene and sterile conditions). The child will probably have a rubber nipple stuck in the mouth, and as soon as baby comes home, he or she ideally will have a separate room in a private house (where Grandma only "visits"). In the church the child is kept away from the adults in a nursery, and in the summer is sent to camp, organized for separation from the adult world. The growing child is bought separate toys and taught to defend them. This isolation and independence is now so ingrained that it runs all by itself by the time the child is a teenager and begins adult life. Of course, the proof of "adulthood" is for a married child to live away from parents. Anyone so unfortunate to have to live with parents is pitied! Thus, a contract-dominated society finds submission and honor to parents a burden that inhibits their rush to greed and materialism. (Thankfully there are exceptions.)

What about the kinship-dominated world? The child is likely to have been born at home with many people in attendance. The child is immediately cuddled and held for long periods of time. Some caring adult who is related to the child is never more than a few feet away—for months! The child begins immediately to sense *interdependence*. His/her subconscious knowledge of regard for other peo-ple is learned immediately. He/she experiences the rewards of caring and touching and being near and sharing. At six months of age in a hundred African societies, that child will be assigned a nurse, who will be an older brother or sister, probably between six and eight years old. That six-month-old baby will soon have an attachment to that nurse (bonding). When the baby is not with mother, then it is with the nurse, who takes the child to mother when it cries. The baby goes with the nurse to play when the nurse goes. The baby also attends many adult activities with

either nurse or mother. African children are allowed in the
adult world as long as they behave. Very few activities are
proscribed from them—including church. Children thus
grow up and are well-behaved because they have learned
adult culture from before the time they could walk.

### TWO VS. SIX

"Civilization" thinks that it has found such a better way,
but in the process has put an almost impossible strain on
the husband/wife relationship. The contract-dominated
society puts all the responsibility of supporting relationships and family on only two pillars—the biological parents
of the children (it's even worse—one-third of all "families"
in the USA are *one* parent families). Here you have one or
two inexperienced people charged with the total responsibility of raising the children. If Grandma does "visit," she's
instructed to keep her nose out of discipline problems.
Grandma as baby sitter will be handed a list of "rules" of
when the children should be bathed, when they should get
up, and what they should eat. Contrast that to a kinship-
dominated world where a family has six or eight adult pillars to hold up the relationships. At least three to five
(some experienced) are charged with raising, nurturing,
and teaching cultural values to the children.

### ...THANK THE OLD MAN

When God intended to give a commandment to his people for their good and for the nurturing of the society, he
had in mind something quite different from the way the
western world views family life, children, and parents.
What a shame that we've allowed our society to drift so far
from God's ideal! Is it any wonder we no longer have a
societal model that we can export to the world in the name
of Christianity? Let's aim this biblical *fifth commandment*
back at ourselves (instead of only at the kids in Sunday
school)! We adults are the only ones who can attempt to
compensate for what our once rural society has lost in

family relationships. Yes, we can restore meaningful relationships by innovation and substitution—without necessarily moving back to the farm!

## Deo Volente

In the short span of time since reaching "majority" (about 35 years), I have noticed quite a shift in emphasis in the United States concerning the symbol "D.V." I used to see it when I was a child. It would appear in personal correspondence at the end of some paragraph in which the writer was proposing to do something in the future, such as take a journey or buy a house or make some important change either physically or ideologically. There was a time in American history when many government officials would include these two capital letters at an appropriate place in their writing—for instance, when talking about the social consequences of political action relating to the future of the country. The French-speaking world of Europe in France, Belgium, and Switzerland still retains, to a greater degree than do U.S.A. Americans, the phrase "Dieu Voulant" (if God wills).

Modern industrial man has "desacralized" much of his world. Western civilization has made giant strides in its knowledge of the human body through medicine and astounding surgical practices. We can change the color of our eyes, alter the shape of our nose, and repair many of the birth defects which only a few short years ago were seen as irreparable quirks of nature. Modern man spans rivers, builds skyscrapers, traverses continents in hours instead of months, and even makes attempts at modifying the weather. It's no wonder that the once-common phrase, "God willing," is quickly being erased from our vocabulary. Industrialized man believes in mastery *over* nature.

This is not so for the vast majority of sub-Sahara Africans, who know the truth of James 4:13:

> Come now, you who say, "Today or tomorrow we will go into such and such a town and spend a year there and trade and get gain"; whereas you do not know about tomorrow. What is your life? For you are a mist that appears for a little time and then vanishes. Instead you ought to say "If the Lord wills, we shall live and we shall do this or that." As it is, you boast in your arrogance. All such boasting is evil. (NKJV)

The great sub-Saharan savannah country, stretching across most of the width of Africa, is the home of millions of people living on the edge of natural disaster. Ecological crises don't come just once in five or six years, but every year, often punctuated by death and real famine. Before modern medicine reached this country, as many as six out of ten children did not live to be two years old. And still today the expected life span in the countries of Senegal, Mali, Burkina Faso, Niger, Sudan and Chad hovers around a mere 45 years. In one of these countries, with eight and a half million people and a land area the size of the state of Montana, there are only two hospitals that have an operating room. There are only ten ambulances in the whole country! The average annual income is less than $230 per year. These people have not yet taken "Deo Volente" out of their vocabulary.

> There was a man who was cultivating his field. The work was almost finished. Someone came by and greeted him: "(Ne tumde) I see you are working."

> He responded: "(Naaba) I see you see me working."

> The visitor continued: "Today, if God wills, you'll finish your field."

The farmer responded that it didn't depend on God. "If God wills or not—today I'm going to finish my field." The visitor walked on and the farmer kept working.

In a short time the farmer looked up and saw an antelope limping badly on a broken leg crossing his field. As he watched, it tripped and fell. He said to himself, "Oh, oh, look at what's here!" He ran and started to wrestle with the antelope, using his hoe as a weapon. But the wounded antelope was too quick for him, and every time he would strike he would miss and hit the ground. WHACK WHACK, missed again. WHACK WHACK WHACK. The antelope could run well enough on three legs, so while running and wrestling, the man found himself far away from his field by the time the antelope escaped. When he got back to the field, the sun was down. The worker went home, and his footsteps went "buda buda buda buda" as he left. He didn't make it when he said that, "If God wills or if God doesn't will, I'm going to finish the field."

When he got home, he told his family he would finish the field the next day; but as he sat down on the ground to eat his supper, he placed his hand on top of a scorpion. The poison pained him all night. In the morning his hand was too swollen, and he still couldn't work in his field.

If cornered, modern man will also agree that the future is not all that certain. He will admit this if you question him, but his day-to-day actions belie the consideration that his grandparents had for fate and the "will of God." What a remarkable contrast between the average West African and the average North American consciousness of the scripture in James 4:

12.  Antelope.

For what is your life? It is even a vapor that appears for a little time and then vanishes away. (NKJV)

We will quote this scripture at funerals—won't we?

## Olungawema

Its color is orange in Denver—blue in Dallas—red in Oklahoma City. It's made of foam plastic and measures about four feet tall. It's a rubber hand with the index finger the only one extended, and its purpose is to announce from over 100 yards away that "we're number one!" It symbolizes a growing American preoccupation. *Number 1* was even the title of a best-seller which openly extolled the validity of the hedonistic, materialistic philosophy that defines this society's measure of success.

The Protestant work ethic, with its heavy emphasis on individualism and equality of opportunity, leads naturally to an achievement-oriented posturing of our youth through a highly quantified educational system. In it, *activity* is more important than *attitude*. We've got the numbers to prove it! As mentioned above, western society stresses hyperindividualism. This spirit of assertiveness is indoctrinated into children at a very early age by a social value of rewarding autonomy. Early in life, self-centeredness is taught to the child and seldom questioned. This can be illustrated by the way each child is encouraged to decide for himself, develop his own opinion, solve his own problem, possess his own objects (and guard them well), own his own property, and, generally, to see his own world from the point of view of the self "ego." Please understand. The writer himself has been a very high achiever and doesn't mean to disparage out of hand a common ethical value recognized for its positive traits. But there *is* another element that sub-Sahara people add to the balance of double image on the subject of achievement. In our land, early childhood consciousness records these themes with purely individualistic goals: "Aim high and you can do anything," "Make up your mind," "God helps those who help themselves," "You can do it—go out there and get 'em!" Consequently, an individual in the west has less fear to take personal responsibility and risk (as one person) than persons in perhaps any other place on the globe.

Other societies, including those in West Africa, see western man as possessing an inordinate drive to "win"—even at the expense of his brother or family members. When Frank Sinatra sings "I Did It My Way," or Sammy Davis, Jr. sang "I've Got To Be Me," the average American is so lulled by an achievement-oriented society that he sees nothing unusual about this attitude. Once our society's heroes were known for courage and/or character. Today they are more likely to be adept at sports, acting, or music irrespective of personal behavior/character. At the crossing of a certain white line on a field, or the jumping high in the air and "dunking" a basketball, the "sports-hero" participates in a wild cultural dance (upraised arms, extended index fingers drawing circles in the air symbolizing unexcelled superiority over all competitors). Immediately the crowd joins in this frenzy with the chant, "We're number one—We're number one—We're number one!" Is it any wonder that the great American pathology (number-one-itis) creates an environment in which the words of Jesus in Matthew 20:26-27 sound shocking? "*Whoever wants to become great among you must be your servant. And whoever wants to be first must be your slave.*"

Americans have a story about the tortoise and the hare. West Africans have one too, called "Olungawema." It too involves animals.

There was a great famine, and all of the animals of the jungle were gathered together around an enormous tree. The branches of the tree spread way out in all directions making the only good shade in the region.

**13. Tree Named Olungawema.**

Many of the other trees had died because of the drought. The tree was very tall and its bottom branches were many meters above the soil. The trunk of the tree was so big around and covered with barbs that no animal could climb it. The tree was laden with precious fruit, and the animals had all gathered because they were hungry.

One of the characteristics of this tree was that no fruit would fall unless someone called the name of the tree. The animals had been under the tree for days trying to remember the name. Hunger increased. No one could remember the name. The animals held a council meeting and decided that the only one who could remember the name of the tree was the wise old monkey that lived in a mountain cave. They decided to send their most *powerful* representative, the elephant, to go up the mountain and ask the wise old monkey. So the elephant set off. When he walked, he went, "Sagalem, Sagalem, Sagalem, Sagalem"—all the way to the mountain. It took him one whole day. When he arrived, he asked the old monkey, "What is the name of the tree?"

The old monkey said, "The name of the tree is Olungawema."

The elephant started back. After many hours, he could see the tree in the distance. He became very excited and happy at the thought of releasing all the fruit which would fall for his friends who were so hungry. In fact, he became so excited that he did not pay attention to a big hole in front of him. He stepped in it (and because an elephant is really very clumsy), he fell down, and rolled over on his back. When he got up and shook his head, he could not remember the name of the tree. Upon arriving, all of his animal friends said, "Try to remember. Try to call out the name of the tree." So the elephant said, "Obumaguma," but the fruit did not fall. "Ohumbamuba," the elephant said, but no fruit fell.

The animals were now really getting desperate. In conference, they decided to send their most *regal* representative, the lion, to also go to the mountain to ask the old monkey the name of the tree. The lion set off at a lively pace, going, "Puush-lipp, Puush-lipp, Puush-lipp." It didn't take him as long as the elephant to reach the mountain, where he asked the old monkey: "Great monkey, what is the name of the tree?"

"The name of the tree," said the monkey, "is Olungawema."

Hurrying on his way back, the lion became very thirsty; so he thought he would quench his thirst at the crocodile pond (one only drinks water there at night when the crocodile cannot see well). Because the lion was so thirsty and didn't think he could arrive back to his friends without a drink of water, he quickly ran to the edge and lapped up a few tonguefuls. Immediately, three great crocodiles rushed him, frightened him, and splashed water with their powerful tails. He realized he had forgotten the name.

Upon arrival, his friends were sad at the news, but encouraged him to try to remember. "Ologahuga," called the lion. Nothing fell. "Obugalinging," tried the lion, but the fruit remained motionless way up in the air, tantalizing all the starving animals. They looked up and their mouths watered, but there was no fruit.

Many of the animals were very weak now and could hardly raise themselves. A quick council was called and they decided to send their *fastest* representative, the impala. But, just as his predecessors, he couldn't retain the name during his trip back.

The next day many of the animals were so weak they couldn't lift their heads. No one had any ideas. Despair and gloom laid thick in the jungle. Finally the turtle said, "I'll go."

Everyone who had enough strength—laughed! "It would take you a week to get to the mountain and a week to get back," said the animals. But no one else volunteered. So, the turtle set out. "Hugg-a, Hugg-a, Hugg-a" is the way he walked as he set out to the mountain. When he arrived, he asked the old monkey the name of the tree. He was told that the name of the tree was "Olungawema." The six days back to his friends were dry and hot and tortuous, but at every step the turtle took, he repeated the name of the tree (and because his steps were so slow, he had time).

Nevertheless, in repeating something over and over, thousands of times, a slight variation sometimes creeps into the mind. So when he arrived back at the tree, his first attempt produced no fruit. The animals didn't even ask him to try again. They had no faith in him. Many of them were now unconscious from starvation. The turtle was very, very weary. But he gathered all his strength and tried one more time. This time he said it, "Olungawema." The tree quivered, then shook. Tons of fruit came tumbling down in great heaps on the ground. The animals who were able quickly awakened and stirred their weak comrades and the feasting began. The jungle was full of joyous noises. The jungle was at peace.

Funny stories, indeed! The U.S.A. vintage (turtle and hare) and the African version are very similar. Too bad they aren't taken more seriously, as they illustrate sound teachings of Christ. The West African world, not being so fixated on measuring systems, can easily see that the kernel of truth that Christ is teaching his disciples is that the *measurement system of this world is not to be used for rewarding those who would work in his kingdom.* Just as those who had expected to be paid more for having worked 12, 9 or 6 hours were disappointed (Matthew 20—story of householder and workers), so were all the jungle animals who placed their faith in the most powerful or the most noble or the quickest.

Jesus doesn't say so directly in the story of the wages paid the laborers, but indirectly he is telling us that if God has a priority, *quality* takes precedence over *quantity.* It would be incorrect to assume, however, that quantity does not count. It only has a lesser priority.

When we read Christ's parable of the talents (Matthew 25) or his parable of the sower and different kinds of soil (Matthew 13) we tend to interpret them from the filter of mathematical minds. In the latter we are amazed that he calls "good soil" that which produces 60- or 100- or 30-fold. If something that produces 100-fold is good, how can something that produces only 30-fold also be good? In the former Jesus said to the one bringing 5 talents (which he doubled to 10), "Well done, thou good and faithful servant" (v. 21). How could he possibly say those same words to the second servant who only started with 2 and brought 4 talents? Can 10 and 4 *both* be "good"? From our quantitative minds, we think Jesus meant, "*Much* done, thou good and prosperous servant." We like that. We can measure it. We can weigh it. We can touch it. It is tangible, concrete. It involves numbers that we grew up with.

The exact minute of our birth is important. The weight, the length, the precise birth date is important. The exact number of days (weeks, months) from birth to first teeth we find significant. And the social consequence of numbers once a child starts school is staggering. There he succeeds or fails, is accepted or rejected, by numbers. Most of the elements contributing to his self-worth and social worth will depend upon the right numbers for the following 12 years, at least. Terms such as "bell curve," "the mean," "the mode," "standard deviation," "percentile," represent words of worth. Is it any wonder that the muscles in the index finger of western man grow strangely strong as he finds every opportunity to raise that finger (holding down the others with the opposing thumb)? A lifetime is spent calculating, planning, scheming, working, just to be able to lift that finger in the ultimate symbol of conquering, arriving, succeeding!

This sign, the raised index finger, used to be a significant symbol of communication and mutual identification in early Christianity. It embodied the idea of the victorious Christ who conquered through submission to show the one way to God. The meaning has now become the opposite. Achieving man clambers up on top of the heap and shouts with shining eye and radiant face, "I've done it! I'm number one!" But Jesus still says, "The first shall be last and the last shall be first" (see Matthew 20:16; Mark 10:31; Luke 13:30). The African knows that the prize often does not go to the swift, and that those expecting rewards often don't get them. There is another system at work—the system that says *being* (attitude, perseverance, faithfulness) is more important than *doing*. The first is on a higher priority in God's mind because it includes the second.

One can *do* without being, but one cannot *be* without also doing.

## A Look at the Birds

Therefore I tell you, do not worry about your life, what you will eat or drink; or about your body, what you will wear. Is not life more important than food, and the body more important than clothes?

Look at the birds of the air; they do not sow or reap or store away in barns, and yet your heavenly Father feeds them. Are you not much more valuable than they? (Matthew 6:25-26).

Two birds predominate in West African thinking. They are the hawk and the vulture. These birds, however, symbolize opposite things. On the savannah, the hawk or eagle is a robber who competes for the African's protein food supply by preying on baby chickens. The vulture is seen by the West African as a peaceful passivist. This, I recognize, is quite different from the way the west generally sees the vulture. Americans see this bird negatively as an animal preying on the disadvantaged. "He eyed him like a vulture" is indicative of that sentiment. We can excuse modern man living in northern climes for being misinformed about the life habits of a bird that lives largely in the tropics. Vultures are not predators but nature's "clean-up crew" sanitation department! They only feed on carrion. The west African sees the vulture in a positive light of a functional animal who is passive before the forces of nature and dependent upon *fate* (much as many Africans themselves are). Thus, all across the sub-Sahara people relate positively to the vulture and his lifestyle and negatively to the hawk. Americans, too, would have a different view of the hawk and the eagle if they lived on the edge of natural disaster like many West Africans.

The story to follow about the vulture and the hawk draws attention to a North American social value that embraces our economic system of capitalism. We value a strong personal assertiveness, the spirit of competition, and a general willingness of society to subjugate nature to our own economic advantage. These are cultural norms for our country. No one should see these characteristics as being inherently bad. They are simply values we have used to become the leading industrial nation of the world. In that process, however, we have turned a deaf ear to the Lord's teaching in the passage in Matthew 6 quoted above.

West Africans have an advantage of insight here, because they have not been mentally programmed from infancy on through college to manipulate the forces of nature, compete with their neighbors, or act independently of family restraints to gain "success." The animistic world of West Africans is based upon a sense of total dependence on a supreme being and an interdependent philosophy about one's neighbor. Instead of acting to dominate nature, they feel subjugated to it because they are vulnerable agriculturalists living in a hostile environment. They associate with the vulture, who is also completely dependent upon nature. These heroic people do not associate with the aggressive hawk (in the story to follow) who takes nature into his own hands.

> The hawk and the vulture were sitting on a tree branch together. They were both very hungry and the vulture said, "I am very hungry—and—hey—I really want to eat, but if God doesn't kill—I don't eat. However, if God kills, I'll eat."

> Then the hawk said, "No way—I am sitting here and I am very hungry and I am going to eat now regardless. Even if God doesn't kill, I'm going to eat."

> They both sat quietly and watched a partridge come out of the field. Cautiously, she had left the field and was now out in the clearing. The hawk said to the vulture, "You see the partridge—I'm going to have it right now. You said you don't eat if God doesn't kill—I eat with my own strength. Just watch—I am going to eat her."

**14. Vulture and Hawk.**

The partridge had made her way to the middle of a clearing and was standing near a dry stump. The stump had been broken and cut and was standing out of the ground with a sharp jagged edge. (A person would have to be careful not to step on it to avoid injury.) As the hawk flew down to the partridge to kill it, he flew with great speed (foooom). At the last minute, the partridge ran and flattened herself against the stick—so instead of landing his claws into the partridge, the hawk rammed the jagged stump instead! As he crashed into the stump, his feathers flew in all directions and he broke his neck in the process. He lay there gasping his last breath as the vulture flew down from the tree and landed near him.

The vulture looked at him and said, "Hey, what is the matter with you?"—as he gouged out one of his eyes. "I said that God kills so I can eat—you are my food." The vulture ate his fill and flew back to the tree to thank God.

When the colonial powers of Europe decided in the 19th century and the beginning of this century to divide up Africa, they introduced a lifestyle very foreign to that which they found. Today, Africa's capital cities and large urban areas are bustling with the way of life that the traditional Africans associate with hawks. The hawk said he was going to eat and make a success of it regardless of the powers that be. The traditional West African is amazed at westerners who don't need to consult the spirits or the powers of nature to build a bridge across a stream. We don't consult the shaman before starting on a long journey. We can cut down trees at random, remove a whole hillside with our marvelous machinery, all of this without making sacrifices to the spirits or the powers of nature.

West African Christians, no longer animists (as described above), still retain much "old world philosophy." They say that when Christ said, "Look at the birds of the air: they neither sow nor reap nor gather into barns," He was talking about birds like the vultures, who are totally dependent on the laws of nature, fate, and the sequence of natural events. Living in a less aggressive world they agree with Christ, who would call us away from the tension and worry associated with the world of technology and the accumulation of materialistic symbols of success (and often the resulting health problems of hypertension, ulcers, and colitis). Christ would call us away to a walk of faith and dependence on his provision. What a dilemma! If we were as passive as vultures we probably wouldn't have the fruits of capitalism. But on the other hand, we might discover a quality of life that Christ talked about in v. 26 above: "Is not life more important than food, and the body more important than clothes?" Is it possible that birds could teach us the ultimate futility of aggressively filling our two-car garages with so many things we have to park in the driveway? Is that what Jesus meant in the next verse (v.27): "Who of you by worrying can add a single hour to his life?"

## Notes

1. *Sega lagefo*—literally, waist money or wealth. This belt was composed of strung cowrie shells and would be worn around the hips under the clothing. Cowrie shells were at one time the medium of exchange.
2. A favorite and nourishing drink made from the uncooked flour of millet and ordinary water.
3. This topic causes inevitable pain. I've learned not to speak on it in public in North America. People tell me (in feedback) that they are convinced of its truth, struck by guilt, and overcome with a feeling of hopelessness about change. That "Christian America" can no longer be a model for family values is cause for alarm. We are indeed "post-Christian America."

# 4

# Faith and the Supernatural

There is a great ideological distance between the superstitious world of animism and the scientific world of industrialized society. Emile Durkheim, known as the father of modern sociology, first wrote about this dichotomy which he called the sacred versus the profane (or the sacred versus the secular). In his understanding of European man he wrote of a great shift in values starting with the Renaissance. Like Europeans in the Middle Ages people living in a pre-literate society today generally cower before the world of natural forces (weather, diseases, food chain cycle, procreation, etc.). They label these natural phenomena "sacred" because they little understand or control them. Even in North America one need only go back about a hundred years to a time when our economic base was much more agrarian to note common beliefs we judge as superstitious today. In those days, my great-grandparents didn't have an understanding of germs and antibiotics or even a very good idea of conception and birth. They were surrounded by many dangerous sicknesses. Child bearing was a major threat to life. Without pesticides and commercial fertilizers, a farmer's yield at harvest depended much more on the weather than it does in our modern world where irri-gation and artificial growing techniques make food produc-tion much more predictable. No wonder their world of the "sacred" was much bigger! There has been a recent shift of such things that once were "sacred" to the scientific secular world of miraculous surgery, vaccinations, and automated farming, to name only a few. Our "secular" world has grown while our "sacred" world has shrunk.

Few people would dispute that with a shift of many old values from the sacred world to the modern secular world there has been a parallel shift in religious faith. Atheism has increased as well as a general disbelief in a personal God. Protestantism especially has seen the decay of belief in the supernatural. The truth of Bible stories is in doubt, as well as the veracity of the miracles Jesus performed. Our culture calls this rationalism "enlightenment."

This chapter invites you to step back into the unscientif-ic environment of the scriptures. It is, incidentally, the ide-ological environment shared by most West Africans today. I would be foolish to deny the great benefits of science and technology and don't see them as obviating my bias of the supernatural as found in the Bible. The reader should attempt to see the next three stories as illustrations of how the pre-literate person's world view predisposes him to see scriptures in a simpler way, unfettered by the constraints of secularism (a scientific world view). I invite you to suspend any tendency to literally judge the elements and characters in African stories, much as one would do while attending live theater where drama is not so much meant to be literal as symbolic.

The walk of faith symbolized in the first story, *Lion Dust*, is carried on into the second element titled *Tolerance for Tares*. A tolerance for ambiguity allows great insights in spiritual understanding because reality in life often demands the mix of the good and bad that Jesus men-tioned. It surely existed in the life of the pious Pharisee though he must have been unwilling to admit it. The "purist" of today abhors the same necessary compromise. I couldn't help but include the third element titled *Thomas and "Kiima"* even though it is a quite controversial way of perceiving some post-resurrection events in the life of Christ. I find it valuable because the Africans I know have a much higher appreciation for the story of Thomas and Jesus than we do precisely because their world view allows them a deeper level of understanding.

The last element of this chapter called *Conceptualizing Spiritual Power* is an example of how the linguistic structure of some African languages influences their conceptualization process.

## Lion Dust

Africans on the savannah usually do not have difficulty believing in the supernatural. The world of animism in which they were raised attributes "life force" to ordinary objects like trees and mountains and rivers and stones. Supernatural powers or "spirits" which are believed to actually "animate" (hence the word *animism*) these objects are thought to have special *other-than-normal* powers. This is the world of shamans and medicine men and fetishes and a belief that supernatural powers can be solicited, purchased and controlled. There is no question but that the characters in the Old and New Testament also believed in the supernatural, but, of course, attributed that power to Jehovah.

The western world of science and technology militates against a quick and easy belief in the supernatural. Much of what the animistic world view of Africa allows, we have explained away or have devised a mathematical or chemical formula making clear the intricacies of all of its functions. I would certainly not argue for the advantage of ignorance which breeds superstition in many of the developing

**15. Lion.**

parts of the world. I do here want to reaffirm my belief, however, in the supernatural of the scriptures and my joy at seeing how quickly the many tribal peoples can embrace the promises in the Bible, such as the one in Luke 12:11-12:

> When you are brought before synagogues, rulers, and authorities, do not worry about how you will defend yourselves or what you will say, for the Holy Spirit will teach you at that time what you should say.

In this passage, Jesus is teaching his disciples they need not spend time worrying or plotting or making a graph on exactly the words, argumentation, and style of persuasion needed to effect significant results if they would find themselves pinched in a crisis. If the Master is saying anything at all to his disciples, he's saying, "Learn to tolerate the ambiguity of facing the unknown difficulty, believing in the supernatural powers of the Holy Spirit to help you—having faith that you have already been adequately prepared to deal with the situation. In that context, answers will come."

Our culture here does not teach us how to face ambiguity well at all. We are taught that the way to face crisis situations is in having answers neatly catalogued in advance of the experience. Just as science tends to contradict belief in the supernatural, so our rationalistic mode of life teaches that pre-set answers and strong preparation are the best insurance against the unexpected circumstance in life.

My brothers and sisters in West Africa are much better prepared to venture into uncertainty with faith than are their counterparts in the west. A Kasena preacher would use a story like the following to illustrate the above scripture focused on the topic of faith and confrontation.

> One man had purchased from the shaman a special "magic force" and its name was "yell-pakre tim"

(emergency power). If an emergency came and you had this fetish or power—you would no longer have an emergency. So he carried this amulet on his person in the event of some crisis.

Now, he had this for some time and had not used it until one day he was in the field hoeing with his wives. Across the Sahel came a fearsome storm. It looked black and green, ominous enough to "make a monkey run and leave her baby!" He told his wives, "Listen, tie up the stuff and give it to me and then you run home—I'll precede you there." So the wives tied up their things and left them and quickly took to the path.

About the time that the torrent hit, he was expecting to "take off" and land in his yard; but the "emergency force" didn't work. (He thought that the medicine would transport him miraculously through the air immediately into the safety and familiar surroundings of his own house.) Thus the rain caught him and the tools for working he had agreed to bring—he had to pick them up and run home in the storm and lightning and hail. When he arrived home, his wives asked him what had happened. "Oh, the power is ruined. That's why I'm all wet."

So the next morning he went back to tell the medicine man: "Your medicine does not work." The shaman asked what he had done to ruin it, and he replied that it spoiled or was ruined when the rain came, and he was not transported home away from the force of the storm. So the medicine man said that under these circumstances he must find one more ingredient to mix with the present ingredients to insure that the medicine would, indeed, work at the next crisis. The shaman instructed the man that he must go to where a lion was resting and make the lion get up. Then he must gather the dust that is still warm from the lion's body and then bring him a handful of this dust. He in turn would use it to make stronger medicine.

So the man set out indeed to find a lion. After much searching he found a resting lion in the bush and boldly walked toward him. When the man raised his hand to slap the lion to move him—and the lion let out a roar "HOOO"—, at that "HOOO," the man suddenly found himself back in the security and safety of his yard! The "medicine" was not spoiled after all!

One of the formulas for failure in a crisis is too much dependency on a pre-drawn map or procedure (assumptions) which obscures important cues from the *context* of the situation at hand. In this proverb used to teach Kasena youth about tolerance for ambiguity they are reminded that a storm is not a crisis on the level of "moving a lion."

From northern Ghana and southern Burkina Faso, the Kasena teaching proverb seems to amplify the Master's lesson to the disciples in Luke 12.

The Christian faith walk is especially gratifying, and not a little frightening, for those who dare to walk in lion country.

## Tolerance for Tares

This segment is an amplification of the previous story, *Lion Dust*. In his parable in Matthew 13, Jesus likens the kingdom of heaven unto a man who sowed good seed in his field, and while he was unaware of it, someone came and sowed *darnel* (tares/weeds). Now when the wheat and the weeds sprouted, the farmer's servants asked him if they should go and gather up the undesirable plants.

"No," he answered, "because while you are pulling the weeds, you may root up the wheat with them. Let both grow together until the harvest. At that time I will tell the harvesters: First collect the weeds and tie them in bundles to be burned; then gather the wheat and bring it into my barn" (Matthew 13:29-30).

In the church today there are still many "farmer's servants" who have an overdeveloped "neatness sickness" characterized as an "absolutistic" or a "literalist" mentality. (Some would even be classed as legalistic.) Sociologists who have done personality profiles on ministerial students and clergy have found evidence of some clear trends of high intolerance of others' values. Missionary personnel are also among those who hold convictions very tightly. Those who volunteer for overseas duty are characterized as being very goal-directed. They are willing to leave family and friends and home to live in a cross-cultural environment for the sake of a religious vocation. I do not want to leave the impression that these are the only people who volunteer for missionary service. However, in my experience of knowing missionary personnel from many denominations and parachurch groups, I would have to agree with the behavioral researchers (and my African colleagues) that a disproportionate percentage of those who come to West Africa, while possessing many admirable traits, also possess a low tolerance for letting the weeds and wheat grow together.

Even if the reader has never lived abroad or has never made the acquaintance of even one missionary, you certainly have known people who feel their calling in life is to *root out the weeds* (identify and pull out the offending idea, or behavior, that is found growing in "God's field"). Some people even have a mental list of all the spiritual and material things they find offensive in their colleagues. When you rub shoulders with these people, their list comes pouring out in all of its unpleasantness. This type of

"Christian" really has difficulty with the above-quoted scripture.

The following story would need no explanation in a polygynous culture to illustrate what such a society feels Christ meant when he said: "No, he answered, because while you are pulling up the weeds, you may root up the wheat with them" (v. 29).

One man said, "God has done me in." He was up one morning and sat at his front door. He saw an old man approach.

When the old man came, he asked, "Why do you sit there and make that sad face?"

The first man said, "Look—God has ruined me, and for that my heart is not pleased and I am holding my head in my hands. Just look at this region here. All of those I grew up with have wives. My brother has wives and children and I still sit here with no wife—and you are still asking me? If it is not God, then who has done me in like this?"

So the old man spoke to him and said, "Look tomorrow or the next day, fire will burn the marshland. When the fire burns the marsh, you run over there and wait. Whatever comes out of the fire, you grab it to be your wife."

So the young man got up the next day and went to the marshland. Truly the fire was burning the marshland, and it burned "ZUGUZUGUZUGU." Running ahead of the fire, he saw an old woman coming out of the marsh. The old woman was a leper. Her fingers were missing and her toes were missing and she was running "BIDEM BIDEM BIDEM." He said, "Hey, I don't have a wife, but I don't want you."

**16. Escaping the Fire.**

The old woman went hobbling past, but right behind her he saw two beautiful young girls running toward him. He thought he would catch one and hug her as she went by. But when he got hold of her, she squirmed away, saying, "I'm helping my old aunt. Let me go." So he tried to grab the other one—"I'm helping my old crippled aunt"—and thus they both got away.

In a little while he saw another old woman running toward him. He looked at her eyes; they were both blind. She was struggling in the weeds on both sides of the path as she fled the fire. Again he said, "Hey, I don't have a wife, but I don't want a blind one."

He let her go too, and shortly he again saw two young beauties running toward him. He thought to himself that he would grab one of them and hold on this time. But just like before, both of them squirmed away and ran up ahead shouting, "I'm helping my old blind aunt. Leave me alone."

Thus, the fire consumed the whole marsh and he didn't get anything. The next morning, the day after, he was again sitting in his doorway holding his head in his hands, and he saw the old man returning. The old man asked, "What's the matter, my good lad, that you still hold your head in your hands like this?"

He answered, "When the fire was burning, I saw some young girls, but they didn't want me."

The old man said, "Look, my good lad—that's the way it is. Don't sit there crying God's name for nothing. You yourself know what you saw. You should have taken what you saw. So—don't blubber the name of God for nothing, because it isn't God's fault. You did yourself in."

West Africans have a great amount of tolerance for the idea that to achieve what you want—to get your desire—you must put up with a certain amount of the undesirable! Great philosophers,they! If the young man had helped these old women, those following her would have come along as part of the deal. If he had assisted the blind old lady, he would have gotten the two young beauties also. Because he wasn't willing to put up with the undesirable part, he didn't get his heart's desire either.

People living on the edge of the Sahara Desert have lived too close to physical disaster to be able to afford the luxury of "skimming the cream" of anything. Life contains many undesirable elements. Their philosophy is: Learn to put up with them or you will never get even the bare necessities. The west tries to negotiate this, from its posture of affluence and great personal choice and potential. We find it a real temptation to think that we can grow "pure wheat" without weeds and even without any chaff!

A close inspection of true leaders, whether in business or in the church world, will show that those who rise in maturity and hold a respected place of leadership for a long period of time are individuals who have the ability to tolerate ambiguity—the ambiguity of wheat and weeds growing together.

G.K. Chesterton said many years ago that the real trouble with our world is not that it is unreasonable, nor that it is reasonable. We are the most troubled by the fact that it is *nearly* reasonable, but not quite. Life is not illogical, yet it is a trap for logicians. It looks just a little more mathematical and regular than it is. Its exactitude is obvious, but its inexactitude is hidden. Its wildness lies in wait.

This tolerance for what is not immediately clear is an almost indispensable quality of one who would seek to lead others. This is the walk of faith. When an individual is willing to venture into uncertainty with faith, assured that he/she is able to deal with the ambiguity *in the situation*, the answer to the questions will come. That kind of cer-

tainty—the kind that one needs to face future circumstances of life—does not come by having answers neatly
catalogued in advance of a given experience. (That kind of
action is a formula for failure.) The faith walk means having confidence that one's preparation will be sufficient to
deal with the circumstances *inside the situation* as it aris-
es.[1]

That is why Jesus could say, "Let the weeds grow with
the wheat. We'll handle them when the situation and timing is right."

That's why the West African would say, "Take the old
blind woman to yourself and then you will be able to hold
the two beauties also!"

## Thomas and "Kiima"

We read in the scriptures the account of Christ's walking
on the water to come and rescue his disciples, who were
being tossed by the waves in the middle of the sea.

> During the fourth watch of the night Jesus went out
> to them, walking on the lake. When the disciples saw
> him walking on the lake, they were terrified. "It's a
> ghost," they said, and cried out in fear (Matthew
> 14:25-26).

Our scientific minds in the western world don't give
much credence to the subject of spirits or ghosts—not really. Of course at Halloween goblins are recreated in masks
and special costuming for a largely farcical celebration.
Ghosts and spirits are held by the average citizen to be
something one doesn't believe in *now*. Oh, we will admit
that maybe our ancestors believed in them (at least, that is
what the stories say). And there are still pockets of beliefs
about certain haunted houses or strange phenomena that
come from abandoned property secluded in the woods.

But when the searchlight of scientific research is turned on, the basis of these persisting stories fades away. Science, as usual, triumphs, and superstitions and old wives' fables "can certainly not be held by mature-thinking individuals."

I do not intend in this chapter to prove or disprove the existence of ghosts or spirits! I have never seen one, nor do I know anyone who has ever seen one. The purpose of this chapter is to show that many West Africans *do* believe in spirits (like the disciples of Jesus did) and to explain the way that belief has influenced their interpretation of a passage of scripture that the west would have no way of "seeing."

Besides the walking-on-the-water incident, the belief of Christ's disciples in spirits or ghosts is apparent in the gospels after the resurrection. After Christ revealed himself to two followers at Emmaus, they immediately traveled back to Jerusalem to find the eleven so they could tell them about the episode (Luke 24:36-37).

> While they were still talking about this, Jesus himself stood among them and said to them, "Peace be with you." They were startled and frightened, thinking they saw a ghost.

Notice that Jesus did not upbraid them for their belief in spirits. He didn't say, "Come on now, guys, you know there are no such things as ghosts!" He did ask them why they were troubled and why they allowed doubts to arise in their hearts. And he comforted them:

> Look at my hands and feet. It is I myself! Touch me and see; a ghost does not have flesh and bones, as you see I have" (v. 39).

Some of them still could not believe, so to further prove that he was not a spirit or ghost, he asked for something to eat. In front of them he ate a broiled fish and some honey.

The West African is convinced that Jesus *too* knew that spirits exist by the way he described their characteristics in proving to the disciples that he was not one.

Now we come to the crux of the matter—how scripture is sometimes *illuminated* through African culture. It is the gospel of John's account of this post-resurrection event that allows us the best look at an African interpretation! Saint John tells us that when Jesus appeared to the disciples and the doors were shut for fear of the Jews, he came and stood in the midst of them and said, "Peace be unto you."

> After he said this, he showed them his hands and side. The disciples were overjoyed when they saw the Lord....Now Thomas (called Didymus), one of the Twelve, was not with the disciples when Jesus came. So the other disciples told him, "We have seen the Lord!" But he said to them, "Unless I see the nail marks in his hands and put my finger where the nails were, and put my hand into his side, I will not believe it" (John 20:20, 24-25).

The Mossi traditionally believed in several kinds of spirits. They believe the spirit world is always with them, and that the spirits of the ancestors constantly guide them through life's difficult decisions in the here and now. One of the types of spirit manifestations the Mossi describe relates to a phenomenon that they call "Kiima."

Any violent death (like hanging or falling from a horse or poisoning—any death that is not normally attributed to old age or a slow debilitating sickness) can be expected to be accompanied by a spirit manifestation either immediately before the person actually dies or a few days after the person has been killed.

Consider the following case study conducted in Ouagadougou, Burkina Faso by the author. The African subject speaking is Sibere Baamogo:

**17. Touch and Believe.**

A "tuulle" is what one sees of the spirit world that shows that someone is just about to die. If you see someone's "tuulle" walking through a field and then you look over to that person's yard and see his real person in the yard, you know that in a few days he is going to die! Of course, you will not tell him.

If someone had died a violent death, not many days after you will see another spirit we Mossi called a "kiima." A "kiima" will always be a perfect manifestation of the person as he was before he died. If the person died from a fall from a horse, where his face was disfigured, or in the process of dying his body was mangled in some way, the "kiima" representation of him will be perfect, no wounds, no disfigurations.

Thus the disciple Thomas said, "You guys didn't see Jesus. You saw his "kiima"—and I won't believe unless I can put my fingers in the nail prints of his hands and put my hand in his side."

This Mossi perception of these post-resurrection events really cast a much more generous light on the west's sobriquet: "Doubting Thomas!" How powerful this story is for the African church: "A 'kiima' has no wounds. You tell me you saw Jesus, but we all know he died violently. If it was really the Master—he'll have wounds in his hands, feet and side. Let me not only see but feel those wounds and I'll believe." The Mossi say: "How generous of Jesus—at first sign of doubt of Thomas, he invited him to touch and believe!"

I submit that the above interpretation is certainly as valid as many others one can read in a broad variety of commentaries written through the filter of western culture. Commentaries simply exclude this dimension of understanding the passage through the belief system of the apostles and the Mossi. The issue at hand is not whether the disciples actually believed in spirits, or whether Jesus did, or whether we should now. The beauty of this explanation by Mr. Baamogo is that it shows that by the Holy Spirit God's word is relevant to the people in the context where the Spirit finds them.

If this is truly an example of how the eastern mind is sometimes better positioned to understand the circumstances and hermeneutical truths leading to spiritual illumination, then should not some very sobering questions be asked? How many times has the western church thwarted a closer, truer visualization of God's holy word by imposing our thought patterns and understanding on diverse peoples around the globe? Wouldn't it be wonderful if the western church in all its missionary zeal would learn to *trust the Holy Spirit to contextualize the gospel message into relevant meaningful revelation?* It's starting to happen!

"Blessed are your eyes, for they see."

## Conceptualizing Spiritual Power

Did the ancient mid-easterner think about his body and its function with a different intensity and level of feeling than modern man?

African vernacular languages often refer to philosophical or abstract concepts in very earthy and concrete terms. In a future segment called "Stomachs," we will explain the concept of generosity or humanness in its positive sense. The stomach is seen as the seat of moral faculties. Authors Dixon and Ellingworth see the stomach and other body parts as having great symbolic relation for the African to deep philosophical beliefs and expression.

The most distinctive feature of the stomach, the seat of morality, seems to be its hiddenness, its being inside the body. So, reference to the moral insides speaks of the hidden depths of the human nature.

Morality is regarded as that which cannot be plumbed, but which alone can spring out its own way to reveal itself either in pleasing characteristics which delight others or in bad-tempered reactions which offend others and lead oneself to social misery.[2]

The following series of words in Mori (Burkina Faso) and Ewe (Togo) expression show how language draws pictures to portray feelings.

1) The work "sousaongo" means "a heart that is spoiled," and would be glossed in translation as "sadness." Someone whose "heart was spoiled" is obviously not happy. Thus the word or expression would be used in a sentence such as: "I received much *heart-spoiledness* when I heard of your decision to leave."

2) The opposite of this would be the word "sounoogo." The meaning of this is "heart-sweetness," and is obviously translated "happy" or "happiness." This would be used in a sentence such as, "I have *heart-sweetness* today because of your coming!" (The reader has no doubt seen that the prefix "sou" means heart. It comes from the word "souri.")

3) Working with the same word "sweet" (noogo), there is an interesting meaning derived from adding the word "head," "zougu." Thus, for the word "zounoogo," one gets the concept of luck or good fortune. So if your heart is sweet you're happy, but if your head is sweet, you're "lucky" or well-positioned in the forces of the universe.

Many references have been made in this book to the importance of the individual in western society. Indeed, the spirit of capitalism which produces much of the industrialization and materialism that we have grown so fond of and addicted to would not be possible under an earlier tribal system of communalism and reciprocity of both needs and accumulated wealth. Linguists can't decide whether Anglo-Saxon speech developed *from* philosophical ideas, or whether speech and language helped to determine our social bent toward individualism.

4) The English phrases "I am hungry, I am thirsty," are quite unthinkable in most West African languages. A person's "being" is wrapped up in much more important entities than water or food. Instead of saying that a person IS hungry or thirsty, most African languages reverse the concept and acknowledge the self as being *acted upon.* Thus when he is hungry he says, "Kom n tara mam," translated "hunger has me." I think I could make a case for this line of reasoning and speaking as being much closer to reality than our system, which relates a human want or need to *being* instead of *having.* One might argue that that is a small technicality, but please understand that we are talking about perception and an acute difference in direction of cognition of where the action is and what is being acted upon. This difference runs through many parts of the language, such as "fear has me"—or, in a slightly different direction, "I have 35 years" instead of "I am 35 years old."

The accumulation of this difference of perception might certainly affect the interpretation of a scripture such as Isaiah 61:1:

The Spirit of the Sovereign Lord is on me, because the Lord has anointed me to preach good news to the poor...

When an Ewe or Mossi or Kasena interprets the word "on," he sees it as a much more forceful word. All three languages say "on my head" (meaning my head has been seized). You don't have a cold in your chest—a cold *has you.* This is deeper than just a semantic difference. You don't have thirst, thirst has you. These sub-Saharan people talk of possession. The French or the English expression doesn't say it strongly enough for the visceral sense language of the African.

"The Spirit of the Sovereign Lord is on me." Regardless of the Hebrew implication of that passage in Isaiah, or the special meaning of the Greek translation in the New Testament, when Christ quotes this verse in his home town, Africans hearing in their tongues experience a deeply significant level of feeling. They are *possessed* by God's Spirit to preach, to heal, to announce; and they see it because their language structures have prepared them to feel it on an intense level.

Has my personal belief system rendered me powerless in my scientific pride? Can I be an effective New Testament style witness to do combat with the powers of darkness (Ephesians 6:12)? Have I as "modern man" lost my ability to oppose Satan's realm with God's Spirit whether I confront Satan's power found in animism of the two-thirds world, or the secular religions of rationalism, intellectualism, and humanism of the industrialized world? Many African languages predispose Christians, who speak them, to recognize the power of God.

I also want it to be said of me, "The Spirit of the Sovereign Lord is on me..."

Do I have God's Spirit or does God's Spirit have me?

### Notes

1. For an amplification of this concept see Robert K. Greenleaf, *Servant Leadership* (New York: Paulist Press, 1977), pp. 185-91.
2. Kwesi Dixon and Paul Ellingworth, *Biblical Revelation and African Beliefs* (Maryknoll: Orbis Books, 1969), p. 127.

# 5

# Family/
# Relationships

This chapter is the most sensitive one in the book. It may not be easily accepted by all readers because it highlights the focal point at which the modern North American, so influenced by affluence and industrialization, is at his/her greatest distance from an African brother/sister relative to the value of people and things. Because this chapter may be perceived as cutting or too negative, I must reaffirm my love for my western heritage as well as pride in being a citizen of the U.S.A. Loyal constructive criticism comes from a motive of caring and building up—not destruction. A repeated question asked by our students over the years is: "What is the hardest adjustment you have had to make in Africa and Asia while teaching and working there?" The answer is the subject of this chapter. The adjustment is easy to identify, but one of the most difficult to talk about.

I was shocked when I discovered, through anthropological studies and years of experience overseas, that my North American culture is labeled a *collector* society. Indeed we are great collectors! Many of us have accumulated mounds of "precious junk" that fills every available space in garage, attic, and exterior storage! At one time I thought everybody lived this way. I've come to discover that there are societies in the world where what you *have* is not what determines your social rank, but what you *give away*. These are known as distributor societies. There are tribes in Africa as well as some South Sea islands where a man's importance in the community is determined by the kind of feast he gives and how he distributes his pigs or goats or other objects of value. In such a society, someone who compiles a lot of "things" is suspect, not admired. If the reader does not believe that North Americans are collectors, take some time to analyze the next few television commercials you see. Every commercial has at least two ingredients: a problem—and a solution. The problem suggests you are inadequate in some way. The solution can be achieved in twenty-eight seconds and usually involves purchasing something. We are a consumer society and seldom are we encouraged to consume on anyone but ourselves. Only in the last few years have social scientists been able to analyze what affluence has done for our great culture. We have found a way to legitimize greed and selfishness. This spirit allows the worst of capitalism to free the average North American from the responsibility of kinship. Yes, North Americans are generous and giving. But we now prefer the escape from guilt about our affluence by contributing to the United Way, Salvation Army, or some other *impersonal* system. It's neat, clean, and noninvolving. We give, withdraw into our personal space, free once again to collect more. Under the older laws of kinship structure the law of *reciprocity* insisted that no one member of a family could become wealthy without also bettering the economic status of all other members of the blood line. *You see, I warned you, you might not like this chapter.* An Igbo living in traditional kinship society would not permit himself to become powerful with wealth while all of his family members stayed poor. Brothers don't do that to brothers and sisters (except in enlightened "civilization"). The law of reciprocity says: "I share my poverty with you and I share my wealth with you, whichever economic state I am in."

I can now better understand the accusations that some segments of the Christian church in Latin America are making (liberation theology). This ideology's proponents look at the rich nations of the world and their unwillingness to abide by the scriptural dictums concerning wealth, or to even show personal restraint with consumerism. Because liberation theology as a system is so tainted with Marxist ideology, it must be rejected. However, the west cannot glibly ignore its positions about wealth and pursuit of things (all symbols of power and ego enhancement) without knowing that this spirit will be judged. How much better if we judged ourselves and resolved to take some concrete action to face the difficult question: Has the western church allowed the pursuit of *things* to replace *relationships* with people?

Specifically, in this chapter on relationships we will consider topics such as *Inside the Wall,* the African meaning of Jesus' tender words to his disciples in John 14. Also there are three segments on *Brothers* and *Brotherhood,* which incorporate some actual dialogue from African "brothers." We will also examine how deep feelings are expressed in African languages which convey the high priority placed on people. *No Stomachs* and *Full Stomachs from Distant Friends* will test your ability to understand subtle analogy. You may find their meaning poignantly powerful. Please don't misinterpret my motives for being pointed. I can take criticism if I have led the reader to consider a new thought. I fully intend to cause some pain, but don't want to lose the patient! F.J. Lindquist, a dearly loved professor, educator, and religious statesman used to say: "The role of the preacher is to comfort the afflicted and afflict the comforted."

## Brotherhood and Things

> The Spirit himself testifies with our Spirit that we are
> God's children. Now if we are children, then we are
> heirs—heirs of God and co-heirs with Christ, if indeed
> we share in his sufferings in order that we may also
> share in his glory (Romans 8:16-17).

Christ is not so much "chief" for an African Christian as
he is "elder brother," as if he were his own flesh and
blood. The African Christian can see Christ as the man in
whom God lives. No one should take alarm at this emphasis on the humanity of Christ, because Jesus Christ in his
glorious incarnation truly epitomizes what it means to be
human. Because many African Christians can see the deep
humanity of Christ, they are able to see how the church is
the "great family" of which Christ is the head and the elder
brother—and somehow God himself—all wrapped in one.
This brings Africans to a clear perception of the unifying
influence of the Spirit of God, which allows them to tran-
scend tribe and clan and associate themselves with the true
body of Christ.

As a person from the west, I had to learn (and am still
learning) that many of my attitudes about things or objects
are really very carnal and unscriptural. Brotherhood in
Africa, as we are describing it in these chapters, liberates
the individual soul from the damaging fixation on material
objects which enslaves my native world.

Traditional African social structure is a network of interdependent, interpersonal relationships. Sad to say, these
priorities are fast disappearing in Africa's capital cities, yet
for the vast majority of the people in West Africa's developing countries, the social security system is still based, as it
has been for centuries, on kinship networks in community
and covenant. Interpersonal relations impacting individual
behavior are thus encumbered with a much higher invest-
ment for success in Africa than similar behavior would be

in the west. Here we have compensated for lack of social concern with depersonalized and institutionalized systems of life insurance, fire insurance, tax-paid police force, Medicare, health insurance, the United Way, etc. These fine institutions, which we all value highly, nonetheless isolate by depersonalization. No longer do we have "people with names caring for people with names." The following three small dialogues are actual quotations of my interaction with West Africans (both Mossi and Ewe) on the topic of brothers and things. The first is around the Mossi concept of *friendship rights* (yaredo ne taaba).

*Zabre Sidibe*   White man's custom and our custom are not alike. A "brother" could come into my house and take something—and not ask me or not ask my wife, and she wouldn't say anything. But if it's the Europeans I know, this couldn't happen like that. Even an elder brother doesn't have the right to come in to a European's home and do as he likes. But with us, we like friendship and peace with each other.

*Author*   You mean, real brothers or those you consider brothers in Christ treat objects and things differently in your country?

*Zadre Sidibe*   Yes, if I want something in my brother's house, I'll just name it—and he'll give it to me, even if he needs it or if it's very expensive. Now that's because of love and we say that it is a "friendship pact" that was made with each other which permits that kind of a situation.

*Author*   Oh, now I see! This is what allows you to come and "borrow" your friend's motorcycle

> without asking him and it doesn't seem to upset him.

*Zabre Sidibe*  You're learning, you're learning! The white man will come up front with words and he'll ask, "Are you still my friend, Sidibe?" But that's shameful for an African to talk so directly. If I want to know if you're still my friend, I won't ask you—I'll just come and use some "thing" that belongs to you and then I'll watch your face when I return it.

Does this not give us a little glimpse of how Christ and his community of "brothers" (disciples) might have lived? Think of some of his words about things and objects: "So do not worry, saying 'What shall we eat or drink' or 'What shall we wear'" (Matthew 6:25). Or consider the admonition, "Don't say to your brother, 'Be blessed and go in peace,' when you're not willing to satisfy his needs with your things" (James 2:16).

A very astonishing portion of scripture comes to mind from Matthew 25 where the Master talks about sheep and goats and the last judgment. Fifteen verses in this chapter concern themselves with what people do with objects, and the real lesson is not in "things" themselves, but *attitudes* about things. Jesus talks about the giving of food and drink and clothing and wraps it all up with the phrase, "I tell you the truth, whatever you did for one of the least of these brothers of mine, you did for me" (v. 40). In Christ's day and still in Africa today, it was and is impossible to separate brothers and things.

Listen to Mr. Baamogo Sibere:

*Baamogo Sibere*  For us black people—like if you and I that are sitting here together—if we are with each other and if we were black people and I was your friend and you were my friend, I mean really good friends! Even if you came and saw that my sandals were lying there like they are now—you could take them. And if I came looking for them and said, "Where are my sandals?"—and they'd say that you had come and taken them—that would be okay. Truly, there is no problem with that.

This conversation with Mr. Baamogo suddenly stirred a deep memory of an occurrence that had happened a few years previously with an African colleague and fellow administrator working together in a pastors' training school. This gentleman and I became the best of friends, but once in a while he would come into our kitchen unannounced, go into the refrigerator, and pour himself a glass of cold milk. This was later reported to us by our kitchen help. I quickly asked Mr. Baamogo about this *strange* behavior (for me, a westerner). We picked up the dialogue:

*Author*          What about this affair with the milk?

*Baamogo Sibere*  Since he had come to know that you and he had become one—he knew that someone could not come between your friendship anymore. That was the reason.

*Author*          And to do this—was the proof symbol of friendship?

*Baamogo Sibere*  Exactly! He would later ask your kitchen help what your reaction was to his action.

*Author* (sadly)  I'm afraid we didn't do too well.

*Baamogo Sibere*  He was looking for a "seal" of friendship.

*Author*　　　　　I've still got a lot to learn!

*Baamogo Sibere* Don't worry—he probably forgives you.
　　　　　　　　To begin to learn new things is hard.

A highly educated Ewe from the capital city of Togo articulates extremely well the point of this chapter:

*Mr. Tchevi*　　　When friendship is quite deep, sometimes one begins to doubt the strength of this friendship. So to find out if this is a friendship that is like brotherhood and will last even until death separates one or the other, sometimes a game or a thing is done to find out how to react toward the friend through this staged game.

It could be that I have a bicycle and my friend does not have one. Anytime he can ask me for it and I'll give it to him. One day, however, I leave the bike at home and he comes and takes it when I'm not home (he knows when I'm home and he does this on purpose). He also knows that I'll come and need it soon to make a trip—even that evening, but he keeps it for two days simply to know what will be my reaction, my speech, my thinking. After these two days he brings it back and says, "Oh, my brother, my friend, you see—you were absent and I took it behind your back which was not too good, but I needed it and took it." He thus excuses himself.

If our friendship is really true—I'll say,

"Oh, that makes no difference—it's okay. What is yours is mine and what's mine is yours." After this exchange, the person will excuse himself and promise not to do it again. He then leaves. Now he'll ask those around me to see if I said something to them about this affair before he brought it back. If my friend substantiates what I told him, then he'll know that our deep relationship can continue or if our friendship was hypocrisy.

Have you ever thought to count the number of times that Jesus himself related things and objects to relationships? In retrospect, I can't believe how blind I have been. I've been living in a world that compartmentalizes and isolates *brothers* from *things*.

## Breathing and Brothers

The reader will recall that these small segments are dedicated to the pursuit of knowledge and illumination of the scriptures through the eyes of West African culture. Consider the scripture in John 20, which causes great consternation to the North American. The setting is immediately after the resurrection when the disciples are gathered in a locked room discussing the great events of the crucifixion and burial of their master. Jesus appears:

Again Jesus said, "Peace be with you! As the Father has sent me, I am sending you." And with that he breathed on them and said, "Receive the Holy Spirit" (John 20:21-22).

The North American is taught not to breath on people! We experience difficulty when we come within the range of smell of another person, especially if we do not know this person or are not on close terms with him or her, and particularly in public settings. There seems to be an intensity and sensuality about a "too-close" encounter that overwhelms the American's senses and makes it very difficult for us to pay attention to what we should be hearing or saying or doing. A good example of this would be the behavior of Caucasian North Americans in a crowded elevator. When their sense of personal space has been violated they tend to stop talking, hold themselves with rigid muscle control, and stare at the changing numbers as the elevator moves past the floors! Experts in the study of proxemics (use of personal space) tell us that most North Americans who come from basic northern European stock are known all over the world as the great "non-contact people." They have a need for a lot of personal space relative to most other people of the world. These same experts tell us that North Americans spend great sums of money to isolate all their personal body odors from each other by deodorant sprays or substitute scents. We place a high social value on someone who does not "smell." Our language is full of little sayings, such as "he breathed down my neck," which show great discomfort when two people are in close proximity and in undesirable circumstances.

One needs only to look at the television commercials of this land to see a true picture of American values relating to personal space and smell. We no doubt have a greater preoccupation with "bad breath" than the rest of the world put together! I do not mean to imply that all of these values are improper or somehow inferior; I am simply trying to bring the reader to an awareness of the reality of what exists. If our culture has a set of values about breathing and smells, etc., which is really quite extreme compared to the values of other regions, then how are we going to react when we read a scripture such as the one above about Jesus "breathing" on his disciples?

Would you believe that many African people associate

breath with friendship and brotherhood? How would you react to news of one African tribe who believes there is special "life force" in spittle? When a newborn baby is first displayed for the neighbors, they all spit on the newborn—not in derision, but in an act of utmost vulnerability and giving. The animistic world believes that strong medicine can be made from spittle, and thus they symbolize a supreme act of acceptance to the new member.

Can you imagine a society which has learned to greatly depend upon the body's chemical messages as an important source of information concerning another person's attitudes? West Africa, as well as the middle east, apparently recognizes that there is a relationship between disposition and smell. Americans are perceived in many places of the world as being distant and aloof and non-committal because we are seen as not willing to participate in intensive communication between people—communication that involves a close enough proximity while speaking so that not only are all the words exchanged, but also some of the subtle smells of the body and breath! Bathing another person in one's breath is a common practice in many Arab countries and also between very close friends in West Africa.

The following excerpt from a transcription of actual dialogue with two official drummers from the Mossi emperor's court will illustrate my contention that mutual vulnerability and trust can lead to behavior much like that described in John 20.

After many hours of unstructured, relaxed visiting with these men, they began calling me "Ga Soaba" (friend in whose house you sleep) and using the word "Budu" (tribesman). In thinking about the context where I had noted this phenomenon happening previously, it suddenly became apparent that this had only happened when in conversation I opened up and became "touchable."

It's true—the thing that we Africans really want, the

main thing, is love and respect for each other. I am
not talking about God's love because God's love goes
way beyond people's love. I'm talking about you coming here and talking to us and wanting to learn about
our ways; and in the process, you have found that
what we really want is your love and understanding.
Your love and understanding that we can now feel
makes us bigger inside. We, then, in turn cannot only
increase your knowledge, but cause you to feel our
love as well in return.

I think Africa has taught me that the gesture that Christ
made when he "breathed on his disciples" was not incon-
gruous with the cultural expectation of deep brotherhood.
It may even have been a symbolic act of sharing and giving
and mutuality that would far surpass an attempt to communicate the same feeling through verbalization.

In spite of over a thousand years of contact, westerners
and Arabs and those from the middle east still do not
understand each other. Americans come back from the
middle east telling how they are immediately struck by the
overwhelming smells, the crowding, and the high noise
levels in that society. If mideast society in the time of
Christ was anything like it is now, then the African might
have something when he says he doesn't have much difficulty with the idea of Jesus breathing on his disciples. The
African thinks that it was simply a sign of brotherhood—
deep brotherhood.

Most of us aren't even remotely aware of all of the vari-
ables of culture that have formed our thoughts and values.
It is only normal, then, for Americans to view Christ's
behavior toward his disciples with a strange sort of repul-
sion or at least perplexity, stemming from our own hidden
set of assumptions. Have my culture's subtle beliefs about
attitudes concerning smell and breath become a barrier
against more effective witness? I don't want it to be said of
me: "He went ten thousand miles to reach those people,

but was unwilling to go the last ten inches." O God, may they say of me, "He breathed on us and gave us a gift–the gift of himself."

## Brotherhood

You don't compete with your brother.
All brothers are not equal.
When West Africans read the word "brother" or "brethren" in the scriptures, their perception is eastern/kinship/communal in focus.

Proverbs 18:24 says, "There is a friend that sticketh closer than a brother," but the understanding of that sentence from east to west contains more differences than similarities.

EDUCATION

One of the obvious and most appreciated ways that the west can help Africa is in education. Many Americans and Europeans are teaching in different places on the continent. In this classroom setting (western teacher–African students), a certain phenomenon happens repeatedly which is a source of much consternation to most western teachers. This phenomenon is related to the West African's concept of the word "brother" or kinsman. Even though imported education systems are based upon a competitive spirit where each member of the class competes against each other (and the two-thirds world tolerates these systems for the sake of the rewards of having a western education) the "developed world's" shallow concept of *brother* is not quickly accepted in the host country. When a western teacher is giving an oral exam or questioning the class of Togolese students, a scene like this is often repeated:

The teacher asks Kojo on the front row, "Who was the first president of France's Fourth Republic?" If Kojo doesn't know and gives a long pause and shakes his head or is just silent, it's unlikely that the teacher can get anyone else to answer that question, even though they all may know the answer! The teacher may be heard to remark that his class is very stupid or isn't motivated to learn, etc., etc., when in reality the teacher does not understand that the *higher priority* of not shaming a brother is more important than having the right answer.

That kind of classroom behavior is a far piece from a society which teaches children the joy of learning to excel at the *expense* of someone *who does not know the answer.* Do you recall the scene in your childhood classrooms? Hands will be raised and eyes sparkle in excitement as the children who *know* bounce up and down in their seats trying to get the attention of the teacher as they seek recognition.

THE FAMILY OF GOD

What does it mean to *belong* to a community of siblings in a kinship society?

— To be linked by a vital union of *life force,* which unites both vertically and horizontally the living and those departed.

— It means that individuality is not forfeited, for each person receives this vital force. But, rather than exploit his/her uniqueness, each one submits to collectivity because each individual draws from the same source and thus senses an interrelatedness.

— This power of life that unites siblings creates a reciprocal action. Not only does the power reach out and "seize" the siblings collectively, but in turn it is "seized" by the brothers and sisters.

— Life is not destroyed by death. There is no lasting break between life and death, but continuity exists between the two as in concentric circles.[1]

— Like the ancient semitic tribes of the Old Testament, people of the clan believe that their departed ancestors' spirits are still with them and influence them. Thus, the dead constitute an invisible part of the family and, in some ways, a most important part!

— That in all the major transitions of life (birth, marriage, social status, death), prescribed ceremonies are performed which celebrate the perpetuity of community.

— The vital word is "incorporation." The family or clan is a *whole*. They share the same blood, and this vital link must be preserved and protected at all costs.

No matter what theological difficulties westerners may have with some of these concepts, the fact remains that West Africans interpret the scriptures relating to the word "brother" from the historical matrix of their own cultural filter. I believe a strong case can be made that the western world of hyperindividualism (which often encourages alienation from the community) has insulated itself from the herd instinct that kinship peoples experience. We hardly know how to appropriate the examples that the scriptures use in talking about the community of believers and moral responsibility to members of an extended family. The communal action of Christians in the book of Acts is too often seen as something that might have been good for that age—"but you certainly don't expect *us* to act that way about *our* property; isn't that fanaticism?"

I submit that kinship cultures are formed to resonate with the apostle Paul when in the book of 1 Corinthians he discusses the body of Christ and the vital link through participation in the whole by individual members who together make up the brotherhood. One might say:

> According to this way of thinking, to exist is to participate in a mystic power, essence or reality ... the individual cannot distinguish, within himself, between what is his very own and that in which he participates in order to exist.[2]

I may not have clearly communicated what I feel about the chasm between east and west on this topic of brotherhood. But surely if the reader has made a sincere attempt, you may have a new (or more empathetic) understanding of how a West African Christian might perceive the message of Saint Paul in 1 Corinthians:

> For we were all baptized by one Spirit into one body— whether Jews or Greeks, slave or free—and we were all given the one Spirit to drink (1 Corinthians 12:13).

## Full Stomachs from Distant Friends

Personification, the art of clothing inanimate objects or animals with personality or the characteristics of a person, is not uncommon as a speech mannerism. The people from the Africa I know use personification with great skill. The hostile savannah country running underneath the Sahara Desert is a harsh land where survival is a priority that cannot be ignored. Very few functions of a person's life are unrelated to the intense physical task of keeping body and soul together. It's only natural that many of the metaphors used by savannah people are linked directly to that physiological struggle.

There is a very short story of the granary who talks to the humans who own him. The field also joins in the conversation. This dialogue explains quite well a rather ambiguous verse found in Proverbs. The book of Proverbs is not the easiest portion of scripture to understand, because it is often couched in a type of speech from an ancient day when enigmatic utterances were highly rewarded.

> From the fruit of his mouth a man's stomach is filled; with the harvest from his lips he is satisfied (Proverbs 18:20).

Seeking a literal translation is probably not the best way to understand this particular proverb. Nor would the clear meaning of the following story become apparent by a precise scrutiny of each word. It's a conversation between a granary and a field:

> The granary says that from where he sits (his opinion), his friend is in the bush (uninhabited area). His friend is the field. They want to see each other, but they can't. Now the field said that his friend is at home, it's the granary. They will, however, get together somehow, they say. The field and the granary have a friendship, but they don't see each other. Truly, they have friendship. Like this—something goes from the field to the granary. Again it goes from the granary and into the field. But they say—to see each other is difficult.

The relationship of the mouth and the stomach and the granary and the field are similar, even though they are not directly connected. It's what they have in common (the activity and circumstances that serve as a linking bond) that establishes their relationship with the *natural order*. In the case of the field and the granary—envision the hard work represented by the common link between these two "friends": hoeing, planting, cultivating, protecting, worry-

**18. Granaries.**

ing, praying, sacrificing, harvesting, threshing, carrying, protecting again, rationing, saving, selling, saving again. All this is represented by two friends that never enjoy each other—except at a distance. They are, however, very mindful of each other's role. Some of the best relationships exist at a slight distance, through either mutual consent or natural circumstance. From the granary come the seeds that plant the field. From the field come the seeds to fill the granary, and so the circle is complete.

From the fruit of a man's mouth (his words) his station in life or status is established in the eyes of his peers and superiors. If his "mouth fruit" is good and intelligent and sometimes cunning, it builds him a house or a station in the community of people. This allows him enough peace and security to work (whether hoeing and planting, or running a machine shop, or selling automobiles, or working in a mine, or tending a profession), which in turn allows him to fill his stomach from the proceeds of what his "mouth fruit" allowed to happen. Thus: "with the harvest from his lips he is satisfied." So the lips and the stomach are friends. The stomach gives sustenance to the body, which allows the body to exist so the lips can keep the status or station in life intact.

The overriding idea here could be summed up in the word "interdependence." God's word has never agreed with the individual who would "go it alone" at the expense of neglecting or ignoring other members in the body. Christ gave us this model: the vine and the branches—"without me you can do nothing" (John 15:5). The apostle Paul reinforced this model: The eye cannot say to the hand—"I don't need you" (1 Corinthians 12:21).

May the Lord help us to see that to become "a building fitly framed together" (see Ephesians 2:21; 1 Peter 2:5ff), we need to understand the relationship between the lips and the stomach and the granary and the field.

I once saw a bumper sticker which read: "I love humanity—it's people I can't stand."

**19. Making Mush.**

## No Stomachs

It has been my privilege to have traveled in 17 African countries and also to meet and interact over long periods of time with many of the indigenous national church administrators there. After visiting for many hours and gaining the confidence and trust of these brothers of the church, I've often asked (very delicately) the following question about cross-cultural relations: "What is your greatest criticism of western missionaries?" Naturally, in the western and central African custom of politeness, a probe of this nature cannot be asked quickly—nor can it be answered until a particular conversation has progressed toward mutual understanding and trust. And all such words must be lubricated with humor.

Now, the answer to that question is rarely ever given on the first attempt. It must be ferreted out slowly from many innuendos and indirect hints, until it's finally distilled to the kind of direct response that we as linear-thinking westerners seek.

The almost unanimous response? "Westerners don't have stomachs." This answer, as uncomfortable as it may be for us to hear, is the door of understanding that helps us to see, through their eyes, some verses of scripture that talk about body parts and organs as related to the human soul and psyche:

If there be therefore any consolation in Christ, if any comfort of love, if any fellowship of the Spirit, if any bowels and mercies, fulfill ye my joy, that ye be like-minded, having the same love, being of one accord, of one mind...let each esteem other better than themselves (Philippians 2:1-3, KJV).

Put on therefore, as the elect of God, holy and beloved, bowels of mercies, kindness, humbleness of mind, meekness, long-suffering; forbearing one another, and forgiving one another . . . (Colossians 3:12-13, KJV).

It's interesting to note that in the later translations of Paul's epistles to the Philippians and Colossians, the word "bowels" has been changed. It connotes other things for our generation. The word was originally used to mean compassion, intense visceral empathy, and the deepest feeling from the seat of the emotions. So for many reasons, the King James usage of this designation of human anatomy has rightfully been changed to conform to modern meanings.

Just this week an African church leader was visiting America for the first time. He was almost in a state of shock, being overwhelmed by the affluence and the ease of life, locomotion, and communication that he found. "What impresses me most," he told me, "is the people. They all look as if they're running in their sleep. They have no faces." And, of course, he was right from his perception; for here we are, sitting alone as we cruise along in our metallic cars, daydreaming on our buses, working in our office, or walking along the streets. We seem to be withdrawn from the world and hiding behind blank masks.

Much of his world and indeed a great portion of the globe is still as it was at the time of our ancestors three and four hundred years ago when the King James Version was modern speech. Life was a much more *conscious* experience. Then, when you drank water, it meant tasting your own water from a well that you had dug yourself. Now, you turn on a faucet and water appears from some unknown place. Illuminating a room was lighting candles which you had made yourself. Now you flip a switch and light mysteriously arrives from only God knows where—often the power company itself is not certain. Even only a hundred years ago, eating meant tasting food that you had grown yourself and then cooked at home. Now we seldom know what we are eating or where it has come from. Stop and think of the number of necessities of life being made for us or done for us that are anonymous. They come from someone unknown, from somewhere else, and the only part we play is to pay out money in exchange. The rural African today seldom pays out money for these commodities. Instead, he knows the source and the ingredients, and realizes they are the result of his everyday life. This gives him the satisfaction of self-security and self-vitality and a sensitivity (gut-level awareness) with which Occidentals have lost touch. Has the pollution of affluence and congestion and automation and lack of purpose so changed our moral fiber that we can go abroad and perform the *acts* of compassion, good will missions, aid programs, educational programs, etc., and still be walking around "without stomachs"?

Listen to the way one African informant describes how "people without stomachs" tend to speak.

If we Africans want to speak something, we don't allow it to be said directly. Our speech will curve off or be hidden and finally arrive at its place. But if it's you Europeans, well, you don't fear "head-eating." That's the reason that you don't hesitate to "puncture the eye." The reason is that you whites speak straight only and not bending. But with us, we didn't learn that way. If we see a problem and want to speak about it, we begin by detouring the person little by little until finally we arrive and get to the head. That's why we say, "If you don't own the mushball, you don't break off a big hunk."

This informant has had much contact with Europeans because of his education in French (the official language) in his own country, plus education in Belgium and subsequent association with Europeans and Americans in the Protestant church in Burkina Faso. He told me of a specific true incident when he had been publicly accused of a

**20. Sensitive Young Man.**

wrong-doing in front of 300 of his compatriots. The accusation had come from a European and, though later proven false, was the cause of a drastic change in the African brother's lifestyle.

> I can tell you clearly that when he spoke what he did it killed me while I was still living! If it had been a Mossi speaking those words, he would have known the detour around which the words followed, that perhaps—even though I didn't like them—I could understand the meaning. The words then would not have been on fire like the ones that burnt me. Now, it's not to say that to speak in circles is not to speak of the problem, but the compassionate artistic speaker will accomplish his task without ruining the person's heart. To speak straight like that is a gunshot that can kill people on the spot.

I believe that part of Black Americans' understanding of the word "soul" relates to their non-definable, non-systematized, non-intellectualized, visceral level of cognition that is really described quite well in Paul's admonition to "clothe yourselves with compassion, kindness, humility, gentleness and patience" (Colossians 3:12).

I have sat with African "griots" as they recounted and sang oral history at official religious ceremonies. These traditional occasions demand that the past be made visible by the recitation of the "world order" through proverbs, songs, and semi-secret sayings that represent the mythology of the tribe. When asked how they remember all those lines to be repeated without error, they'll grasp their stomachs and say, "It's all kept right here."

When Jeremiah speaks for Jehovah and says: "I the Lord search the heart, I try the reins" (Jeremiah 17:10, KJV), he is using a word meaning *kidneys*. The Hebrews believed the kidneys were the volitional aspect of human will, "where man makes up his mind." Stomach talk is sensitive.

It possesses an "other" awareness that is deeper than just intellectualizing.

When I am accused of lacking a "stomach," I'm in trouble, because *interpersonally* I need a big one!

## Inside the Wall

Let us look at an interpretation of John 14:1-4 from the "old world."

> Do not let your hearts be troubled. Trust in God; trust also in me. In my Father's house are many rooms; if it were not so, I would have told you. I am going there to prepare a place for you. And if I go and prepare a place for you, I will come back and take you to be with me that you also may be where I am. You know the way to the place where I am going.

It's unfortunate that in the King James Version, the word for "rooms" or "dwelling places" is translated "mansions." The word "mansion" reinforces the idea of the way the structure of the family has evolved in the west—which is misleading to the underlying intent of this passage. Western family structure is drastically different from that which existed during the time of the Old and even the New Testament. West African structure through the extended family is much closer to the model that we see in the scriptures. Don't misunderstand—West African structure is not perfect. Only parts of it are useful as analogy.

A mansion is an entity by itself. One doesn't build a series of mansions sharing common walls like a series of row houses! This is why the later translations of "rooms" or "dwelling places" is much closer to both the exact meaning and the intended meaning of the original in my opinion.

I am contending that Christ repeatedly used the family

**21. Father's House . . . Many Rooms.**

and its interrelationships (the Hebrew model) in his teachings because they present a good analogy of the relationships that he wants us to have in his body and to his and our Father. I submit that the mental image the average westerner has of the word "father" or "brother" today is vastly different from the perception of those terms at the time Christ used them in his modeling (teaching).

Christ's reference to heaven in John 14 should not be related to *riches* and *things* (mansions), but to relationships. In a "thing-oriented" materialistic culture such as North Americans enjoy, we tend to see the teaching of Jesus through individualistic eyes—according to our understanding of family structure. American marriages are ideally neo-local. The couple will "set up their own home." In fact, North Americans believe that any arrangement other than a neo-local household is unfortunate for the newly married pair. Most modern westerners and especially U.S.A. Americans frown on any three-generation households—even when as individuals they may have had pleasant experiences growing up in them.

Westerners opt for the conjugal family instead of a more extended larger family unit. Now, while that structural difference itself is great, its significance and effects on children are even more weighty. The world views of two unrelated children growing up in these two different environments differ greatly. In the extended family, the relatives act as though they also possess the infant and can jointly control him. In the conjugal unit, the child's other relatives act as though they are mere spectators while the infant's own mother and father are in complete control of "raising" him or her. The western model is characterized by individualism and self-reliance. The child's discipline and control are almost exclusively in the hands of the biological parents until the child is older. This is not so in West Africa and in most of the Orient. Earlier chapters have already pointed to this mode as being one of mutual dependence. In that mode, generally four or five adults will share in the upbringing of the same child. In that system each person is not his/her own master, whether aged 7 or 70; and this child's actions and destiny are tied to the parents, ancestors, clan members, and descendants. That kind of a family structure sits on many pillars—instead of only two (or *one* in one-third of current U.S.A. families).

## What Is a Brother?

Imagine with me how differently the two systems would perceive the word "brother." Let's follow the matter of discipline and inter-relationships a bit more closely.

The average North American woman is a *guest* in the house of her daughter-in-law. She is not supposed to give orders to her grandchildren or in any way to contradict her daughter-in-law's orders. If some family emergency brings her into the younger woman's home, she is still supposed to strictly obey the younger woman's method of operation. It would be expected that the younger woman would leave a list of when the children are to go to bed, whom they are to play with, and what they are to eat and wear. Now, to interfere with that order would bring about an accusation that mothers-in-law hope to avoid. (Of course, in reality, they do sometimes succeed in "interfering.")

Conversely, in traditional Africa (as well as China, Korea, etc.), the older woman maintains her position of authority, even in her daughter-in-law's house, and is much like a mistress over the younger woman herself. The main reason is that her daughter-in-law very likely has been living inside the compound since her son brought her there in marriage. But even if the mother does not live under the same roof with her son and his family, she is still expected to oversee the welfare of her grandchildren and thinks nothing of overruling her daughter-in-law when she so desires. Now, the younger woman might resent this, but no one would criticize the mother-in-law for doing it. The father-in-law has even more authority. Thus, children grow up with multiple authority figures, not just two, or, in the rapidly disintegrating family structure in our country, often only one.

The cornerstone of the North American nuclear family is the husband-wife relationship. This is not so in the family structure of the Mossi and the Ewe (and most other tribes in West Africa). The cornerstone in these extended families is the father-son relationship (or uncle-nephew in a matrilineage). In these African nations, households do not "come and go" with marriages as do our households. In our culture, the neo-local American household propagates itself and dies rather than dividing and continuing in multiple versions of the same old components. A son grows up in America and proves his adulthood by separation. A young man grows up in a Mossi family and proves his worth as a son by being *included*. The father shows the whole community that he appreciates this son by making a place inside the wall for his son's new wife and their children. Divorce is a dire threat to the North American household, because of its narrowly defined cornerstone. In much of West Africa, the only thing that can reasonably be called a "broken home" occurs when sons move out because of a "wicked" father, or the father expels them for their insubordination or independence. A wife's or husband's leaving cannot "break up a home." The larger family has custody of the children.

The power situation in a father-son based household is a balance of power between fathers and adult sons. This situation greatly increases the power dynamic between brothers, making that relationship a much stronger bond than in the west. The power situation in a marriage-based household (such as in the U.S.A.) is a balance of rights and duties between husband and wife. This greatly weakens the relationship between brothers. In the husband-wife household, the sibling relationship is of minimal importance. In the father-son household, the brother-to-brother relationship is of maximum importance. An African woman acquires a firm place in the household because she is the indispensable producer of children. Thus, the authority structure of the household and its continuity are to be found in the father-son relationship (or the mother's brother-son relationship in a matrilineage). This is a much closer model to the biblical pattern than the one our culture has taught us. The greed of materialism has torn us apart. We may not like that old model, and it would be futile to suggest we return to it in this society. However, more exact interpretations of this and other scriptures about the family are easier for Africans because of their socio-temporal proximity to Bible days.

These are hard words for industrialized nations and their shattering family traditions. The writer is torn by the decline of family values in North America and Europe *and* the insensitivity of the church which often does little to publicly oppose the slow drift to secular values. West Africa's or Asia's family traditions are not Christian and certainly not models themselves to be emulated because of serious flaws too complex to examine here. These traditional cultural family structures, however, contain glimpses into the past with elements similar to the Hebrew world, and thus are like a lens through which to uncover insight useful for our purpose in *Double Image*.

When Christ, the older brother, says to his disciples, "I go to prepare a place for you," the African sees this as a place in the family—*inside the wall*. This is a secure place (not material, not mansions, not individualism, not separateness). Christ is talking about human relationships of care and interdependency. The African hears Christ's words, "that where I am, you may be also," to mean intention of nearness, tenderness—an inner embrace of care and love and support leading to great security.

"In my Father's house you are to be included. I'm going to make a place for your status, for your position, for your belongingness. We're going to include you in the family.

We're going to make you one with us. We are all going to be brothers and sisters and submit ourselves to the Father. We're going to prove our love to him and for each other by obedience to his will. Don't be troubled. I'm leaving you now, but I'm going away and will work on your state of being—as a part of the family *inside the wall.*"

## *Notes*

1. Dixon and Ellingworth, *Biblical Revelation,* pp. 138-39.
2. L. Levy-Bruhl, *Carnets* (Paris: Presses Universitaires de France, 1949), p. 206.

# 6

# Communications/ Word Power

Tony Schwartz, author of *The Responsive Chord*, suggested to the communications world a few years ago that the west has a five hundred year literacy bias which has led to linearity in world view. This literal print bias is brought about by the high status of literacy in our culture. By "literacy" we mean "understanding knowledge as pieces of information in a printed fixed form with words following one another, left to right, on lines that proceed down a page."[1] For over a hundred years anyone who was not "literate" according to this definition was the object of discrimination. This increased the way our society valued the linear process. Our language, Schwartz says, shows a marked dependence on linearity in the word choice that signifies clear thinking and even proper behavior. We teach our children to "toe the line...keep in line...walk the straight and narrow." We also say that someone who "follows a clear line of thought" is a good thinker. And if someone really understands another person, we say he can "read him like a book." Our logic has been the logic of print where one idea follows another. "Circular reasoning" is synonymous with unacceptable logic, and everyone knows the futility of "running around in circles." Our linear bias, I contend, makes it very difficult to understand people from pre-literate auditory cultures where the spoken word is still the only word. Some biblical literalists are confused when they discover that when John's gospel says, "In the beginning was the Word," it refers to the spoken Word and not the written Word. It wasn't written until much later. I agree with Schwartz that a society that depends on auditory communication for the exchange of messages will organize its world in a very different way from our own. This is an issue that few Bible scholars address. Naturally, unless they have had communication dialogue with pre-literate peoples, they would be limited in their capacity to perceive the point of this chapter. Maybe a seed can be planted here which will bear the fruit of investigation.

We can only speculate on the "literacy" rate of the culture at the time of Jesus. With the only portable writing done in manuscript form (copied by hand), it is highly doubtful that literacy as we know it was very high. Records from early Greek and Roman periods would substantiate that hypothesis and even literate people who could read and write in that age would constantly be interacting with a predominately oral/aural society.

This chapter has seven segments. In the first, called *Drum Talk*, oralness is introduced in a way that is probably quite unique so as to further clarify oralness from linearity. The second segment, called *Second Agenda*, will explore the importance of indirect speaking about which North Americans have an aversion. These first two segments will serve as an introduction to the next two which are titled *People, Names and Power* and *Word Power and Naming* where the central theme of this chapter takes on substance. The next two sub-titles are humorous stories that are variations on the theme. The last sub-title, *Power Encounter Through Naming,* encourages the reader to let African culture broaden his or her understanding of *power* in the name of Jesus. His name should not be seen as a magic formula, but rather as a substance around which faith can fasten. How exciting to believe that God would call any of us as his servants to a power encounter. "For our struggle is not flesh and blood ..." (Eph. 6:12). A Spirit-led believer and witness can not only be victorious in his or her personal life, but by faith can appropriate the power of God available for spiritual warfare!

## Drum Talk

Many tribes on the West African savannah use a special round drum made from the hollowed out, gourd-like plant called a calabash. These drums vary in diameter from 12 to 18 inches. The circular hole cut in the top of the round gourd is covered with a goatskin held on by leather straps which are fastened at the bottom with an iron ring. The drum takes much skill to play. To make it sound properly, a particular "finger slap" must be employed using the full hand and action of the wrist and arm. This gives the proper percussive energy necessary to maximize the excellent auditory potential from the dimensions of a round sphere.

Traditionally, only members of the drummers' clan were allowed to play these instruments. The drums had religious and ceremonial significance to the tribes' maintaining of the universal order and a guarantee of human and earthly productivity. It was believed that both were necessary for the survival of the tribe. Any important chief always had two or three official drummers who would play the above described calabash drums. A second style of drum was also used. It was a two-headed drum strung over an hourglass-shaped wooden log and held under the arm when struck.

Westerners are amazed to discover that African peoples can use the drums to talk to each other, send messages over long distances (their own telegraph system), drum out a

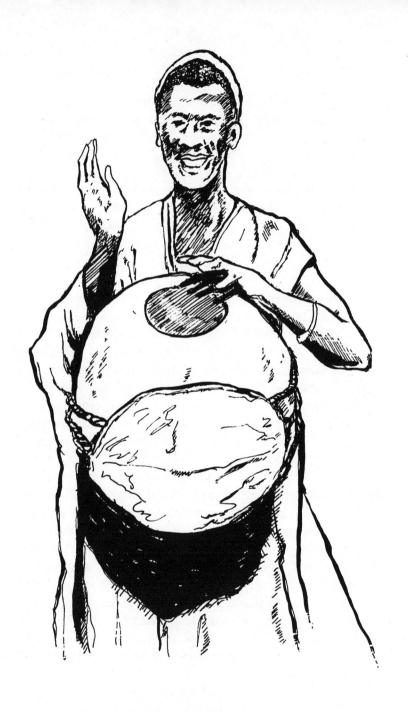

**22. Calabash Drum.**

code understandable to the average citizen, and yet drum out a more secret code understood only by the chief and the members of his court. The writer has spent scores of hours conversing with drummers about their craft. I have made many electronic recordings of the actual cadences, employing a simultaneous oral translation by another drummer, who puts into an African vernacular language the "content" of what the drummer is saying through his drumbeats.

I came to an amazing discovery. I could not understand "drum talk" until I could shift my mind away from the literal, lineal, print orientation of my western system of knowing and understanding.

I had been so programmed by the ABCs, whose letters make up words which must be placed in the correct syntax (word order), that I chafed at the drummer's inability to drum according to *my* rules. Thus I discovered that my capacity to miss drum talk was phenomenal. I found myself trying to twist and turn and "literalize" segments of auditory symbols (drum speech) to my system of cognition—of which I was a prisoner. For the African, drum talk *does* have order and symmetry, and it simply makes sense. I found it non-precise in the extreme (based on my literal, linear perceptual field). This discovery has shown me that much African oral speech is like drum talk. The message is more a general impression whose essence (content) must be "filled in" by the receiver. It is not that the specifics are withheld from the listener, but simply that *the specifics are not the essence of the message.*

Here's an example of how the African ability to listen to the ambiguity of drum talk and find from it content necessary for understanding prepares him to understand some of the teachings of Jesus that even his disciples didn't comprehend. Let's look at Mark 8:15:

"Be careful," Jesus warned them. "Watch out for the yeast of the Pharisees and that of Herod."

The disciples took too literally the words of Jesus, thinking he was talking about their neglect to bring along a lunch. But Jesus was talking in big globs of deep philosophical truth. The disciples' thoughts were on the literal surface of the matter. Now, there were times when Jesus spoke in innuendos to purposely conceal things from those who weren't following him. At such times, he'd speak to his disciples and remind them that they were special: "Blessed are your eyes, for they see." However here's an instance where he says just the opposite. In verse 18 he accuses them of having eyes and not seeing, of having ears and not hearing, and of not even being able to retain things in their memory. L.M. Hussy describes the disciples' fault, and at the same time defines much of western man's weakness in understanding Christ's words.

> The disciples set about to torture a literal significance from phrases first coined to blast utterly a literal intent.[2]

Now, back to drums. I asked the drummers, "What if a chief wants to show displeasure to one of his subchiefs and express that thought through drum talk—what will he do?" The answer:

> If a subchief does not please the chief, the chief will wait until he himself is sitting on his throne before his subchiefs and elders have gathered around him. When he sees the particular subchief come into view on his way to take his place seated around the chief, he will look sideways at his drummer like this (sideways out of the corner of his eye). He's wanting the drum to talk words. Then the drummer knows, when he gets the eye—and sees the subchief coming—that the chief isn't pleased with him. Then the drum will speak. The drum will say—No one can refuse his uncle. A person

cannot refuse his father. Even if he's planting, go and learn planting. If he's hoeing, go and learn to hoe...

Of course, the chief is not talking at all about planting or hoeing. He's talking about submission to a superior. He's talking about obedience and human relations. The African preacher laughs at the naiveté of the disciples who also misunderstood Jesus. He says that of course Jesus didn't mean to talk about literal bread or even literal leaven. They say he's talking about *provision*. The scribes and Pharisees have a provision that one can follow. It's called legalism and leads one away from knowledge of the Father through religious nit-picking precision. There's also the provision of Herod. His "provision" is not on the right, like the Pharisees, but on the left, through secularism. But the African says, "You see, Jesus is saying, 'Fellas, there's a path that steers between both of these leavens. Don't you remember when through faith and working together we fed 5,000, and how many baskets we had left over? Don't you remember when we fed 4,000, and how many baskets we had left over? Can you really have experienced these things and still not understand what I mean?'"

Drum talk—it's a little bit like using a piece of smoked glass to view an eclipse. *It conceals in order to reveal.*[3] How strange for us prisoners of a literal print bias! The following segment will amplify this thought.

## Second Agenda

Many West Africans think there's more yet to why Jesus spoke "unclearly" in Matthew 13.[4] It has to do with the techniques of *indirect* speaking for the purpose of getting across a message.

One technique of indirect speaking is *third person persuasion*—influencing the attitudes and thinking of someone by using a neutral third party. For instance, an encyclopedia salesperson might use a quotation from some famous personality who has praised the effectiveness and the value of her great source of knowledge (her brand of encyclopedias). She will have her sales pitch either on tape to play for the prospective client, or written out so that when she's in the act of selling, she can use something that seems to come from another source. In this way the salesperson is appealing to the authority of the well-known individual who likes the encyclopedias.

Another form of indirect speaking has fascinated researchers. Much study has shown that pieces of information that are overheard (by accident) are sometimes stronger than those heard directly. Exactly why this happens researchers are not sure. Perhaps a good theory is that when we hear something directly and are confronted by face-to-face communications, we put our guard up, believing that we must resist the speaker's impact by counteracting the persuader's intention with our mental defenses. Conversely, when we hear something by accident, those natural defense mechanisms are not in operation. The hearer realizes that the overheard message was not originally intended for him or her.

Was there some indirect speaking in Jesus' explanation of his rationale for talking in parables? Many Africans think Jesus may have been giving the disciples credit for having better eyes and ears than they really had!

To illustrate this idea, I ask you to consider the setting for the small story below. When the Mossi arrange for the marriage of their children, the act of sending the daughter or bride to her new home is spoken of with the word "kuis." It signifies the act of the bride's family making the initial gesture of "sending home" their daughter into the kinship system of the father of her future children. Also note that African stories often personify animals to mean people (a form of indirect speaking) when they want to speak about very delicate matters. In the story that follows, the hyena is speaking to his daughter, whom he is about to send (kuis) to her future husband.

> The hyena wanted to send his daughter to her husband's home, so he called her and began to counsel her. "Now—when you go to your new husband, when you get there, listen to your husband well and make a lot of food for him. If you fix him meat—give him lots of meat. If you do this, you and your husband will be compatible." While he was counseling his daughter like this, he suddenly said, "Ah—it is my daughter I am advising. If someone else's child happens to hear, it's his sweet ears that permit the information. If someone else's child hears, it's because of sweet ears."

> What was happening was that while he was advising his daughter about being a good wife, his own wife was listening; and it was because of her "sweet ears" that she heard the counsel given to her daughter. Even though it wasn't the wife being advised, the hyena (husband) knew that if his wife would do what he advised his daughter, it would be good for him, too!

For the Mossi, the expression that your ears are "sweet" refers to luck or happenstance. A lucky person is spoken of in the Mori language as someone having a "sweet head."

When Jesus was talking to the multitudes and teaching them about his Father, he often did so by speaking in parables. The disciples sometimes questioned him as to why he didn't speak more clearly and why he spoke in parables. The African sees a connection between the story of the hyena and his counsel to his daughter (and at the same time to his own wife!) and what might have been intended when Jesus turned to his disciples after having counseled the multitudes and said: "Blessed are your ears, for they hear."

Consider the context of this scriptural passage, "Blessed are you for hearing (obeying)—you'll be the recipients of my Father's gifts if you'll learn to see and hear." It may have been third person persuasion way back before we had a fancy term for it.

## People, Names, and Power

A good name is more desirable than great riches... (Proverbs 22:1).

The European stranger visiting Africa will not be told how the hosts use names of people. Part of the reason for this may be that Africans, like all other peoples in the world, seem to think that their own cultural values and assumptions are not only the *right* ones, but that they are universally understood. Consequently, Africans don't know that Europeans use names of people differently, either.

My wife and I often laugh when we remember our futile attempts, during our first years in Africa, to ascertain the couples (husband and wife) who belonged together, but were not often seen together in public. Thus, by normal means of public observation in the west, you might not know who's married to whom unless you would go to their home.

Nor should one waste his time by asking a woman in many African countries the name of her husband. She will never tell you. She'll giggle and put her hand over her mouth in embarrassment, but she won't tell you her husband's name. Traditionally, a wife could be put to death if she repeated her husband's name. During her whole life she must not utter it. The name of the head of the house is so powerful, so sacred and related to honor, that for a wife to repeat the name of her husband, in public or private, was a capital offense. Her place of submission to him (socially) would not allow her to "form the word." Because the wife is not allowed to say the name of her husband, if a son is a "junior" (has his father's name) she cannot even call that son's name because it's the same name as his father. So all of his life, the boy's mother simply calls him "kem yuure," which means "elder's name."

In traditional societies, many African tribes do not name their new babies until after the baby can speak. This means that babies do not receive official names until some time after their second year of life. The reasoning is that a name is so important it should correspond to the particular unique personality of that child or to some event that was seen as significant at its birth or at its conception. To name a baby prior to its ability to speak would be disrespectful *to a name*!

Names of individuals are not used in greeting like: "Hello, John, how are you today?" Names are simply not used easily, even between good friends. A name possesses an aura and an essence of power related to "life-force." One does not quickly pronounce a person's name because of the relation it has to the power of the universe and the interrelated communal spirit of the village or clan. Greetings are given thousands of times a day, but are generally "nameless" and more formal and auspicious than our simple greetings, which are often hollered across the road in passing, like: "Hi, Jean, how are ya?"

When a chief is declared in many West African tribes, a special investiture ceremony is held which includes the choosing of a sacred name. This name is not the name he was given by his kinfolk. (However, he still retains the "ordinary" name, even though it, too, now takes on special significance.) Suppose that a Mossi chief had the name of *Tenkouka*. He probably was given this name because his mother sought conception of a child by sacrificing to the spirits of her ancestors at the base of a kapok tree. She may have made a promise that if she would conceive and bear a son, she would call him Tenkouka (town kapok tree). When Tenkouka becomes chief, the name "Tenkouka" is suspended from usage for any other male called Tenkouka who lives under the chief's jurisdiction. So all the boys and men who have the name Tenkouka will now change their names to "Nabyuure," which is translated "chief's name." So when you hear a mother call for her child (which she is allowed to do if it's not the same name as her husband), and you hear her holler "Nabyuure," you know that his previous name is the name that has been suspended from being used by the community in favor and honor to the chief who bears that name which no one repeats! There is a more important name than that, however, that the highest chief takes in Mossiland. I speak of the name of a Mossi emperor (Moro Naba). The emperor, it is believed, takes on a new name *and* the personality and characteristics of the ancestor who formerly had that name. Here's how it's done.

Each of the past Mossi emperors and their names are related to a separate spear and horsetail switch (for some 15-20 names) which have been preserved since the 13th century. There are something like 37 or 38 former Mossi emperors. These spears are kept in a special sacred hut. At the death of a Moro Naba, a new chief is chosen. At a particular time in the ceremony, he is led blindfolded into this hut, at which time he will choose one of the spears that are standing around the wall of that round hut. He will bring the spear and the horsetail out together, where they will be identified by the keepers of these sacred objects, and thus be given the name of the person who formerly owned these sacred artifacts. The special sacred name now "chosen" must never be repeated by anyone in the kingdom.

This poses a special problem. All of the Mossi history is kept in the memories of griots, or drummers, who either sing or drum out the oral history of the names of all the emperors and their important deeds. Every year a ceremony called "Nabassega" is celebrated, when the spiritual heads of the tribe renew the powers of the earth and its ties with the heavens and universe. This insures the rains for food, and the fertility of the women for preservation of the tribe. At that ceremony, songs of praise and adoration are

23. Spear and Tail.

sung to the spirits of all of the important dead ancestors (such as the dead emperors), who the living believe are not really dead but are part of the "living dead." The spirit of these leaders is thought to influence current events and circumstances and bring good will and health. During this ceremony, drummers drum out the names and the special deeds of all of the previous emperors beginning with the first up to the present. Remember, however, that the present chief has taken (by chance) the name of one of the previous 37 chiefs in the sequence. A singer, or drummer, must be very careful to remember the present "special name" of power and religious significance that the chief holds; and while he is calling out the names in sequence, he must *skip over* the name of the particular chief that the present chief holds! It was a capital offense if he forgot.

In light of all of this, it isn't difficult to imagine how the African preacher can poignantly interpret scriptures such as:

Salvation is found in no one else, for there is no other name under heaven given to men by which we must be saved (Acts 4:12).

...but rejoice that your names are written in heaven (Luke 10:20).

Therefore God exalted him to the highest place and gave him the name that is above every name (Philippians 2:9).

Let me feel, with our brothers, the strength and power and hope that the African believers experience from the promise in the book of Revelation:

Him who overcomes I will make a pillar in the temple of my God...and I will write on him the name of my

God...and I will also write him my new name
(Revelation 3:12).

Can you picture the richness of biblical teaching about
the Old Testament characters who had their names
changed, like Jacob, Abraham, or Naomi? What a great
blessing and depth of perception the African has because
of his cultural background and understanding!

## Word Power and Naming

Because of the West African's concept of word power,
he has no difficulty at all with the fact that God used *language* to bring the world into being. The words *"And God
said,"* used nine times in Genesis 1 in the creation process,
are clearly related through African eyes to God's power
represented by his words.

The traditional world view of the West African ascribes
an awesome and even religious significance to the power
of words. In a previous chapter, we related how the words
of a chief were regarded by the tribe as being strong
enough to either bind or loosen someone from a social
obligation, depending on the context. In this chapter we
want to look at how the distinctively human capability of
forming words or "naming" influences the way West
Africans interpret passages in the scripture that refer to *the
word* (kerygma).

First, consider the supernatural qualities that West
Africans traditionally give to the pronouncing of words or
"languaging." The African divides the world up into categories of forces. The first force would be the force held by
beings who can think and talk and, more precisely, beings
that have command over *nommo* (the special "word"
which is significant to us here).

On a lower level are forces that cannot act of themselves,
but are activated only by the command of *nommo* (a word

of power). Here we have plants, animals, minerals, tools, furnishings, etc. Among these items or objects are certain ones which are seen to be magically imbued with a life-force that is "congealed" and waiting for a command of the magic word of a thinking person (the person who has command over *nommo*). The congealed forces can do nothing of themselves; they have no will of their own. For example, even a poison is not potent until it receives the command.[5]

*Important:* In the hierarchy of forces, *nommo* holds the highest place. Even procreation is not accomplished merely by sperm, but by sperm and word. Thus, the thinking being, able to pronounce *nommo*, is not established in that status by the act of birth alone, but by being designated by a word. For the Mossi, a baby is not a "real person" until he is officially "named." By designation (naming), a tooth becomes an amulet, a carved piece of wood becomes an image. Thus, in all of Africa, all sorcery is *word.* Since the word has such power, everything one says is binding. There is no "harmless" or casual word. The following humorous story illustrates the power of the spoken word of an important individual like an emperor.

There was a man who was called Chief Fiinsi, and this was his real name—Fiinsi. Among his subjects was a man who did not like him, and used for a pretext of his insubordination the fact that he believed that "Chief Fiinsi" wasn't a royal name—and thus, he could not be a true chief. The chief answered that they would both go together to the Moro Naba (emperor) and sit in court and tell this matter to the emperor. They both agreed that whatever the Moro Naba would answer, they would abide by his judgment. If he should say that "Fiinsi" is not a royal name, then they'd know that he really was not a chief.

So they went and greeted the chief and told the Moro Naba: "People call me Naba Fiinsi—and this man says

**24. Emperor.**

that Fiinsi is not royal. Thus we said we'd come and tell you."

And the Moro Naba answered, "What did you say, Naba Fiinsi?"

Now when Fiinsi heard this, he jumped and hollered for joy and said that he'd been set apart as a chief, because normally when a chief is selected by a higher chief he never pronounces the word "chief" (naba). He sets other chiefs apart with a hat and they just "hat" him, and his mouth never says the word "chief." From that day on, Chief Fiinsi never had to worry about his status, because the emperor himself had called him "chief."

Considering the above concept of *nommo*, can you imagine how Christ's words to Satan at the time of his temptation would take on special significance to an African's ears? At that instance, when Christ refused to do a miracle of changing stones to bread, he quoted Deuteronomy 8:3: "Man does not live on bread alone but on every word that comes from the mouth of the Lord."

Creation power, sustaining power, the force of life itself, is mysteriously related to language. Now, some may have theological difficulty with all the implications of this relationship, but to say that God can or should only be conceptualized through the filter of western culture is neither generous nor wise.

## Rooster Eggs
### (or the Power of Words)

There was a day in this country when someone's word was as good as a written contract. In reading early history of the American colonies and accounts of industry and commerce from that period, one glimpses an era where a person's spoken word, given as a symbol of his worth, reputation, and honor, was highly respected. Today we prefer a notarized contract or at least the imprint of a credit card in a machine. We probably do this because it is so much easier to take legal action with written evidence. Our present age doesn't put much faith in "oral contracts." Quips such as "get it in writing" and "make them sign on the dotted line" are symbolic of a change in attitude from putting great faith in someone's word to a day when we put almost none (unless we can record it electronically in the absence of any document).

How then does someone from our generation interpret the words of Jesus in Matthew 12:37?

> For by your words you will be acquitted, and by your words you will be condemned.

This segment would like to give the reader a glimpse into a culture that is still pre-literate (from our print-bias western definition meaning unable to use *writing*). Even though the situation is changing rapidly with advancing educational opportunities, the present literacy rate in West Africa and the absence of a "print" society makes their value of the oral world much closer to that which existed in the New Testament scripture context.

If a society holds that a person's word is his badge of honor, then those words, used even in simple conversation, carry a great weight. If words, however, are spoken by an important person like an African chief, they tend to be immutable and take on characteristics of the law itself. Before colonialism, when an African chief made a pronouncement, the weight of those words could free you or kill you, depending on the circumstances. This, then, is the context in which the following African story is set.

**25. Chief's Court.**

There was a man named Yelkonlingma, meaning "Circumstances will not surprise or overcome me." He gave himself this name and let it be known that the significance of the name meant that no matter what comes—when it looks as if there is no way out—with *words* he would get out of the situation.

The village chief came to hear of this name and its significance and he thought, "All right, I'll come up with a situation he won't get out of." The chief took a rooster and gave it to Yelkonlingma. "Take my rooster and help it to lay eggs." So he took the rooster and went home.

A few days passed. Now, there was a dead tree near the chief's yard, and so Yelkonlingma climbed the tree at night to cut some of its limbs. The chief called out, "Who is cutting wood?" They told him that it was Yelkonlingma who was cutting wood. "Call him." So they called him. "What are you cutting wood for?"

Yelkonlingma replied, "My father gave birth and he said for me to come get wood for a fire (it was the cold season) so the child won't be cold."

The chief asked, "What! How can a man give birth?"

Yelkonlingma bowed with respect and said, "But you gave me a rooster and said to make him lay—he, too, will have trouble giving birth!"

The story shows the confidence that this man had in the power of words to evade trouble. Of course, this could not have happened if the society in which he lived had not respected the cunning use of word power and had not taught him this possibility. Here the person who caused the dilemma, the chief, was tricked into releasing his subject from that very dilemma. A chief's words are the final authority. "How can a man give birth?"

The Ewe tribe of southern Togo believe so strongly in the power of a person's spoken word that if something happens to one's voice while he is talking, they immediately suspect witchcraft. Thus, if someone is speaking or singing and gets a "frog in his throat" or begins to lose his voice, he will say, "Adze le gbe nam" (Witchcraft has me). A polite listener hearing someone choke up or talk hoarsely will immediately say, "May witchcraft not take you!" This points out the importance of words by saying in a tactful way: "Don't worry, witchcraft has nothing to do with your voice problem."

A person's words are directly connected to his worth in society. In both the Mori and Ewe languages, if you want to show how much you esteem someone, you will relate that sentiment to the way he talks. Thus, "To love a person is to love what he says."

For by your words you will be acquitted, and by your words you will be condemned (Matthew 12:37).

## Boudema and the Abuse of Word Power

The last couple of titles are attempting to show the unusual significance that West Africans accord the power of the spoken word as a part of social behavior. Pre-literate societies also treat the *abuse* of word power very seriously—even more seriously than we do in the technological west. Salesmen in the west are generally not legally bound by the exaggerated and sometimes erroneous claims they make orally. Many a consumer has discovered this fact with great disgust and sometimes with sad financial consequences.

The seriousness of the shocking story of Ananias and Sapphira in Acts 5 isn't difficult for North Atlantic peoples to understand. Lying to the Holy Spirit is using words abusively. But we sometimes raise our eyebrows at the quickness and severity of the penalty. In this chapter I would like to amplify the gravity of the Acts 5 account by helping the reader to see it through the eyes of African culture.

> When Ananias heard this, he fell down and died. And great fear seized all who heard what had happened (Acts 5:5).

Ananias had just heard the accusing words of the apostle Peter after trying to deceive him about an amount of money. The significance of this event in the eyes of Africans is the fact that "telling falsely" about a communal agreement or assumption has great social implications. Any kind of telling, true or false, is reciprocal and touches on the vital system of interdependence on which African society stands. "Telling" is related to trust and the nature of communal social security—the only kind available (it does not come with a number on a little card).

Boudema was a mature adult male with a family who lived in a small village on the savannah. He had never attained to greatness nor done anything out of the ordinary to get the attention of his community or to receive praise from his peers. Deep in his heart, Boudema craved recognition. One day he went before his chief with the usual gift showing honor and submission (a chicken or a goat). When it came his turn for an audience, he told the chief:

"I have an unusual request for you, my chief, but I don't know exactly how to ask you."

"Well, Boudema, why don't you just speak up? I think I'll understand."

"Oh—it's really nothing, chief. I think I'll just forget it."

The chief and Boudema then went through a series of verbal gymnastics with the supplicant pretending he couldn't say it for embarrassment, and the chief trying to reassure him that he was at liberty to speak his mind.

The chief asked him: "Do you want me to arrange another wife for you?"

"Oh no, my chief, I don't need another wife."

"Do you want a larger field to farm in?"

"Oh no, my chief, I have plenty of land to farm."

"Well, then, what is it, Boudema? What is it that you want?"

Boudema lowered his voice and leaned far toward the chief and in a whisper said, "I don't want you to give me anything. I just want you to whisper in my ear!"

"Whisper in your ear? Well come up close, and I'll whisper in your ear, you silly man!"

"Oh no, Your Honor, I don't want you to whisper in my ear here. I want you to do it in the marketplace. Here's what I want you to do. The next time you're in the market and many people have gathered and they're all around selling their wares and buying their wares, I want you to stand up from where you sit on your chair in the middle of the market and call out: 'Is Boudema here? Is Boudema here?' Then I will come when I hear you call and I'll kneel down beside your

## 26. Whispering.

chair, and you just whisper in my ear. I'll nod my head and keep nodding my head as you talk in my ear."

"Well, if that's all you want, Boudema, there's no problem. I can do that with no difficulty."

The next time there was a big market, just as he had requested, when the marketplace was full of people, the chief stood up and called out Boudema's name two or three times. Boudema answered the call and came and knelt beside the chief, who indeed whispered in his ear while Boudema nodded and nodded without saying a thing. All of the people in the market who had heard the chief call for Boudema and then subsequently saw the scene of the chief whispering in his ear while he nodded approval and acknowledged the chief's words began to talk amongst each other. "Oh—Boudema has become the chief's confidant." "I wonder what it was the chief was saying to Boudema."

Now when Boudema needed food, he began to go to the villagers one at a time over a period of a number of weeks and he would say, "The chief has sent me and says that he needs a rooster today." The family would unhesitatingly chase down a rooster and give it to Boudema, who in turn would eat it. In a few days he would go to someone else and say, "The chief has sent me requesting a goat." He would receive the goat and promptly turn it into stew for him and his family.

After many weeks, a tattered old man made his way to the chief's yard with a special supplication for the chief. He told the chief how Boudema had come and taken his last sheep, the one he had been saving to sell in the market so that his only grandchild could go to school. The chief was taken aback.

"What? I never sent Boudema to take your sheep, or anything that belongs to you. What is this story?"

Thus the story began to unfold. Over a period of three months, Boudema had extracted 37 animals from different people of the village. Some he sold, some he ate, but all in the name of the chief!

The chief called a village council and all Boudema's deeds were uncovered one at a time and made completely public. He was then given a very severe choice. He could either pierce his own body with a poisonous arrow and die with honor and bravery, or he would be killed by the chief's honor guard. Boudema chose the former, and thus the story ended.

The village so honored the words they presumed the chief had said that when Boudema deceitfully spoke in the name of the chief, he had free access to the material possessions of the village. Let us go back to the case of Ananias and Sapphira. Their words were seen as especially devastating because the untruth affected the material well-being of the community who had pledged themselves to equality in material objects.

Think of the power of the words of a covenant in the Old Testament. Western cultures are amazed at the reason Isaac would not go back on his covenant to Jacob, or retract his words, even though Jacob received a blessing through deceit (Genesis 27).

We marvel at how Rahab could openly lie to protect the spies of Joshua, and yet the "word" of the spies was honored and she and her family were saved (Joshua 6).

Even though obtained through deceit, the oath of Joshua to the Gibeonites was honored (Joshua 9). In fact, that covenant was defended militarily by the whole army because of the power of the spoken word as related to the seriousness of abusing that which had been spoken.

There is yet another aspect of "words" and "power" about which the African world view can enlighten us. Through this window of understanding, let us consider the gospel of Mark in the section to follow.

## Power Encounter Through Naming

Mark's gospel uniquely shows his consciousness of the power struggle between the forces of good and the forces of evil, or God's power and Satan's demonic power. Biblical scholars believe that Mark's gospel addresses the Roman world more than any of the other gospels. With a backdrop of the Roman political and social tyranny of that day, Mark's gospel draws back the curtain and reveals Christ confronting the powers of the enemy.

> "What do you want with us, Jesus of Nazareth? Have you come to destroy us? I know who you are—the Holy One of God!" (Mark 1:24).

Mark remembers that under demonic influence the person revealed the true nature of God Incarnate.

Africans, being traditional animists, are very "other world" conscious. They live with spirit powers. Of course, the west debunks the animistic world and wants to class it all as superstition. We seek scientific reasons to desacralize much of what they think is supernatural. Nonetheless, from their elevated awareness of power against power in all phases of their lives, they attach special significance to the way Mark describes the ministry and miracles of Jesus.

In other separate events in this gospel, similar confrontations between Jesus and demons present themselves. When Jesus confronts these powers, in each case they try to gain an advantage over him by *Word-selection-naming*. "We can identify you—we know who you are," they say in essence. And they *name* him as if they mean to gain power over him by saying his sacred name or title.

Whenever the evil spirits saw him, they fell down before him and cried out, "You are the Son of God" (Mark 3:11).

Up until now I've wanted you to see how the words themselves pronounced by the right people and in the right way can often have great effect on human behavior and on circumstances. Mark seems to imply that the presence of Christ, even without his speaking, forced out certain words of truth. Probably the clearest illustration of this is in Mark, the fifth chapter, where Christ's encounter with the demoniac of the Gadarenes occurs. In the presence of the power of the Messiah we hear the words:

He shouted at the top of his voice, "What do you want with me, Jesus, Son of the Most High God? Swear to God you won't torture me!" (Mark 5:7).

Some anthropologists and archaeologists believe that many of the paintings and wall etchings found in caves from earlier mankind were not essentially an attempt at artistry. Rather, they reflected early man's belief that by tracing or reproducing the likeness of an animal, the "artist" could somehow gain power over the animal by capturing the essence of its life force.

By repeated description, Mark demonstrates a belief held by the common people of Christ's day, *and* also demons, that there was something substantive about precise identification of the Christ using specific words or a formula of words.

It is not my intention to take sides in any current theological contentions about whether the spoken word is more powerful than the written word. Rather, my purpose throughout these pages is constant—wishing to raise the possibility (and advisability) of seeing theological concepts through something other than western eyes. I can hear an African preacher say:

> The demons thought they had the right formula; they thought they could defend themselves by using the most powerful weapon they knew. Identify and expose the Father's plan about his Son. Uncover the secret of who this God-Man was. But Christ would have no part in it. His power from the Father was much more powerful than the secrets the demons happened to have known.

West Africans see that Boudema (above) misused the name and essence of the chief to gain his own advantage. If African scholars are allowed to escape the narrow window of western theology and interpretation, they'll teach their people to believe in Christ's name in a fuller measure than only a magic formula.

God's power and essence cannot be totally contained in words the mouth can utter. Yet no theology—from any culture—should fail to understand the power and meaning of that name. Like Peter in front of the Sanhedrin, we must proclaim: "Salvation is found in no one else, for there is no other name under heaven given to men by which we must be saved" (Acts 4:12).

### Notes

1. Tony Schwartz, *The Responsive Chord* (New York: Anchor/Doubleday, 1973), pp. 6-10.
2. L.M. Hussy, "The Wit of the Carpenter," *The American Mercury,* vol. 5, pp. 329-36.
3. Archibald M. Hunter, *Interpreting the Parables*

(Philadelphia: Westminster Press, 1960), p. 14.

4. See "Ears To Hear," Chapter 1.

5. Jahn Janheinz, "Value Conceptions in Sub-Saharan Africa," *Epistemology in Anthropology* (New York: Harper and Row, 1964), Chapter 4.

# 7

# Little Stories, Big Truths

In keeping with the theme of the first six chapters, the purpose again is to teach via contrast. A polarity of cultures, ideologies, or values will bring into relief or focus ideas that might not readily be apparent without the contrast. The first two segments of this last chapter center around the word *meek* (*Blessed Are the Meek* and *Security Can Afford Meekness*). This word, and its scriptural characteristics, are flat-out resisted in capitalistic North America. My plea is for Christian brothers and sisters to take stock of their status and position as children of God.

Christians should resist the secular world's distortion of biblical values. The western value of productivity and subsequent need for measurement (while good in itself) must not displace a quality of *being* about which God has a priority. A believer's "being" is always more important than his/her "doing"—even though doing should not be minimized or discounted. Rather, doing is a natural product or "fruit" of the believer's status or "beingness."

The third and last segment (*Antelopes, Goats and Greener Pastures*) illustrates that humanity really has many

180

similarities in spite of the differences in contrast the book has been highlighting. Hopefully, these little stories will do more than entertain; may they also stimulate useful truth to the production of fruit.

## Blessed Are the Meek

Nowhere in the New Testament do I have a closer glimpse of the heart of our Lord and Christ than in the beatitudes of Matthew 5. They are greatly misunderstood because their maxims are upside down to the industrialized world. Some in the western church naturally have tried to justify aggression, competition, and assertive behavior by the scriptures. The beatitudes, in talking about the poor in spirit, the meek, those who mourn, the merciful, the pure in heart, the peacemakers, would certainly have a hard time in today's school of economics and business management!

African society, which is traditionally "people-oriented," valuing human interrelationships over materialistic objects, contains within it the ability to perceive the precepts Christ wanted to show us in his teachings from the beatitudes. The beatitudes look "upside down," and, according to Bretscher, the world in its sinfulness has rejected the beatitudes given by Christ because of its upside-downness. For this well-known verse on meekness, it has substituted, "Blessed are the aggressive, for they shall dominate the earth."[1]

This cunning story illustrates well how the West African's culture helps him to get to the meat of Christ's intended lesson:

The hyena and rabbit were going to hunt for eggs. These eggs are those laid by the wild guinea fowl who live in the bush. Walking along, the rabbit found a nest of ten eggs. He shouted, "Oh, look—here are ten eggs for me!"

Then the hyena said, "Oh no, I saw them before and left them here for us to find now." He came over to where the rabbit was, picked up the eggs, and put them in his bag.

As they went along, looking to find more, the rabbit cried, "Ah, here's 20 for me!"

The hyena said, "Put them down where I hid them before. I'll come and get them." So the rabbit left them, and the hyena came over and gathered them. On ahead, after more time, the rabbit found a nest of 30 eggs; but before he could pick them up, the hyena came and said, "Oh no, I was here earlier and gathered them there for us to find now." And he picked them up. At the end of the egg-hunt, the hyena chose two or three eggs and gave them to the rabbit and sent the rabbit home.

When the rabbit got home, he took one egg and broke it and had his wife smear the yolk on his rectum (she broke the egg and put it there). Now, as usual, the hyena's fire had gone out, and so the hyena sent his wife to the rabbit's yard to borrow some coals to start his fire so she could boil the eggs. But when the hyena's wife came and saw the rabbit stretched out and his bottom was all messy and heard him moaning there on the ground, she said, "What's the matter, Brother Rabbit?"

"Oh—I went with your husband to hunt eggs, and when I got home I ate one, and I've *really* got diarrhea."

Well! The hyena's wife went back to her house and she said to her husband, "Hey, my husband—you should not eat those eggs that you brought us. I just saw the rabbit who ate one, and he's got diarrhea." So the hyena got up and gathered all the eggs and put them in the garbage outside the house. The rabbit got up and gathered them!

NOTE: Special explanation for the story should be given. Speaking of body functions such as elimination is not perceived as being uncouth or inappropriate to speak about, even in a public meeting. Most of the developing world does not find it necessary to mask the real world with euphemistic substitutes. We ask for the bathroom or restroom when we want neither to "bathe" nor to "rest!" One other note of significance: guinea hen eggshells are about five times more resilient than hen eggs. Consequently, when the hyena dumped them all out in the garbage, most of them would not have broken at all.

The rabbit's behavior while gathering eggs in this story portrays for the West African the behavior of *sons* of God. Meekness is not weakness—meekness is controlled strength. Meekness is exemplified by the power of restraint. In the story, the rabbit didn't need to strike up an argument every time the hyena lied about having hidden the eggs in advance. In spite of the momentary external appearance, the rabbit knew he would come out ahead. On the other hand, although having the appearance of winning, the greedy hyena would be made to look the fool. Isn't this exactly what Christ tried to teach us about the principles of his Father? The psalmist David saw this and repeatedly sketched the scenario of how good triumphs over evil for those whose hearts are aligned with Jehovah's.

We must insult God when we live upside down and seek

security outside of him. Like the hyena, those who grasp and seek to possess and grab will not prosper. The reason the world cannot be possessed by the aggressive is that it already belongs to the meek, the sons of God, who have it by right of inheritance as the gracious gift of the Father.

"Blessed are the meek: for they shall inherit the earth."

## Security Can Afford Meekness

The characteristic of MEEKNESS heads the list of human attributes that the Creator desires to find in us, his creatures.

The western world often characterizes meekness as a defect, as a flaw in character. The Bible sees it as a virtue.

One can only be "meek" by choice. A person is never just genetically naturally meek. That's part of the misunderstanding North Americans often have of this word.

People who confuse meekness with weakness make a grave error. Meekness is the opposite of weakness—it only proceeds from a base of strength and confidence.

To be meek involves a conscious choice to not take the advantage, even when one has the power and the right to do so.

The beatitudes in Matthew 5 give great insight into the "kingdom culture" by detailed close-ups of the mind of Christ. This is, no doubt, the reason these verses are so poorly understood. The world would say they simply don't make sense. How could anybody be blessed who mourns? How could one rejoice in being persecuted? Who could possibly believe that the meek (according to the standard definition) merit *any* gift, let alone inheriting the earth? These few strange verses point up the glaring fact: Christ's values come from another world! The value system that underlies the beatitudes is upside-down compared with the one that our world view espouses—and I submit that this applies to all regions of the globe.

The following African story illustrating the theme of this chapter is a historical fact. It is an account from the 17th century, from a time when the Mossi people were a very strong political force in the country that is now called Burkina Faso. As powerful warring tribes do, the Mossi had conquered and assimilated many neighbors around them. The other tribal people involved in this account were the Kasena (known in French literature as the Gournsi).

The Mossi emperor (Moro Naba) had conquered the Kasena. He regularly extracted tribute from this powerful tribe to the south that his armies had subdued. One year at tribute collecting time, the emperor made the mistake of sending his son Nabiiga (the prince and heir apparent). When the Kasena saw the heir with a very small entourage of guardians, they overpowered the group and took the prince hostage.

All of his kingly robes were stripped from him, and he was forced to walk around with only a loin cloth. The prisoner was given but one meal a day, and every morning forced out into the fields to hoe. Now, the regal heir does not do manual labor. It is beneath his royal dignity. But the Kasena made great sport of him. The women of the tribe would come by and, as they are so capable of doing, belittled his manhood by accusing him of not being a virile male. The children would come by while he was hoeing in the field and throw small pebbles at him while he worked. This was a significant act of derision.

But to the surprise of all those watching the scene from day to day, the Mossi prince would work and

## 27. Hoeing.

sing. He sang cheerfully and with a loud voice as his back bent to the hoe from sunup to sundown. At first his soft hands bled when blisters broke, being unaccustomed to the manipulation of a short-handled hoe. He lost much weight, but continued to be cheerful and to sing. The elders of the Kasena tribe were much troubled by his singing and buoyant attitude. "How can he possibly sing," they would ask, "since we make him sleep on the ground? We give him very little food, and he is forced to work. Our women and children mock him—but he still sings!"

After a month of this treatment, they finally called him before a council. He stood with only his loin cloth, straight and proud, in their midst. The elder spokesman for the Kasena people publicly asked the Mossi prince about his behavior. "Why do you sing?"

The Nabiiga answered, "It is true. You have taken away all my fine clothes. Everyone can also see that you have made me work, that you give me very little food, that you make me sleep on the ground in a common hut. You have tried to take away all my pride and all my earthly possessions. You have brought me great shame. Now you ask me why, in spite of all this, I can sing. *I sing because you cannot take away my title*. I am the Moro Naba's first son and need not react to your shameful behavior!"

Jesus said it in Matthew 5:5, "Blessed are the meek: for they shall inherit the earth." It is really easy for the sons of God, you know. They don't need to be aggressive and to fight defensively, because the inheritance is theirs. The Nabiiga had learned as a child that he didn't need to covet his father's giving of gifts to the many subjects who would come bowing before him. He did not find it necessary to be jealous of the father's bounty to others around him. Was not everything going to be his? Was he not the heir apparent?

Security is not to grasp for more, but to let everything go. Wouldn't it have been unwise for the prince to show anxiety and distrust about his father's intentions for him? His job from early childhood was to seek the good of his father's kingdom so that one day he would have the mental prowess and correct attitudes of maturity to indeed inherit the mantle of rulership.

When will we also learn to take Christ's words literally about seeking his kingdom?

A rich young ruler came to Jesus and the Lord talked to him about security. Jesus said to him, "Give away what you think is security and you'll find a different kind of riches" (Matthew 19:21). Jesus also said to the Pharisees who came to him, "Let go of the law whereby you dominate others. Let go of the system by which you hold people under obligation to yourselves in the name of God." Security is to trust the Father. That kind of security allows meekness to be demonstrated in human action. How we must, as God's children, insult the Father by acting as if his promises are not trustworthy!

We must indeed insult God when we live by this world's upside-down measuring system and seek security outside of him. Through the example of Jesus we see that, though he possessed very little of what the world around him would call security, he lived a life of security. He taught it. He insisted upon it for others.

The earth cannot be possessed by those who grab for it or who violently try to own it. It already belongs to the meek, the sons of God. They own it by right of inheritance as the gracious gift of the Father.

Blessed are the meek—and blessed are the eyes of those who know that they can *afford* meekness because they have accepted the Father's adoption.

## Antelope, Goats, and Greener Pastures

The apostle Paul wrote of contentment—even from a smelly dungeon. He encourages us, by his example, to be more tolerant and accepting of our present circumstances. Do not all people need this encouragement? In spite of the obvious differences in cultural and behavioral practices in the world (one of the themes of these chapters), the writer here wishes to again avoid any misconception.

I do not wish to imply in these chapters that no *commonalities* exist between western culture and West African culture. For the reader to draw that conclusion would indeed be a mistake. Perhaps the similarities greatly outweigh the differences. In many respects, people are the same. While most of the chapters in this book highlight differences between peoples for the sake of teaching by contrast, this segment would like to show a commonality of human behavior illustrated through an interesting African proverb. This story would be told in Africa in a family setting or in a small group setting where friends gather to exchange wisdom and participate in communal sharing of thoughts, ideas, and social values. This type of interaction is a great tool for the socialization of the young in traditional African society.

BACKGROUND
There is a small antelope that the Mossi call a "walaga." It is known by the word "dyker" in English. The walaga is only one in a species of dykers, all less than 18 inches high when adult, generally weighing less than 20 pounds. Because they are relatively easy to kill and their meat is extremely sweet, the walaga is an immediate target for anyone who sees him.

The walaga saw a goat out in the bush and said that he wanted to go home with him. The goat said, "Don't come to Man's yard, because Man's yard has much trouble."

The walaga retorted that the goat has many advantages. Not the least is that goats live in herds, but the walaga must be alone for safety. "Besides that," said the walaga, "look at our plight. If a woman sees a walaga, she says, 'Kill it, kill it!' Even a child will begin to run and throw things at us. Thus we have to hide from people, and we can't group together in a herd or we'll be more easily seen. But look at you!" said the walaga. "You bunch 10 or 15 together and you can visit together as you graze. So you see, Man's yard is better than the lonely life we live in the bush."

Then the goat answered and said, "Okay, think about this. In the Man's yard there are gifts to the in-laws, gifts for the dead, and gifts for brideprice. All of these gifts are blood gifts, and they take most of these gifts from among the goatherd."

But the walaga said, "Nonetheless, the yard is better, and the bush is 'kill and be killed' every day." So thus the walaga followed the goat to the Man's yard; and because the goats were many, he just hid by walking in the middle of the group when they went home at night.

During the night the man of the house called his son. "Go get a goat to make a sacrifice." Well—the young son came in "swoosh" and grabbed the walaga's hind leg and pulled him out of the goat shed. He pulled him by the hind leg across the yard and stuck the leg in his father's hand, who was waiting with a knife. (Remember, there are no electric lights, and at night most things are done by feel.) The father grabbed the

## 28. Sacrifice.

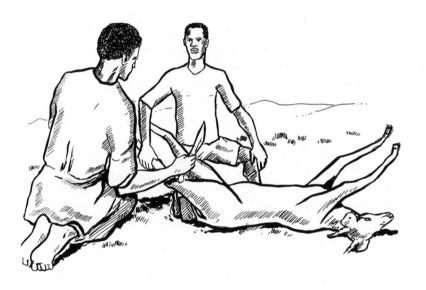

hind leg and said, "Oh no, leave that one. That's a nanny goat. Catch a billy goat and give me."

So the son carried the walaga back to the goatherd, released him, and caught a billy goat, who bleated "Waeh, waeh, waeh" as he was dragged across the yard. The antelope's heart was still pounding as he heard the blood running, "furdurdurda–furduda." This walaga lay quietly and trembled as he listened. His goat friend said to him, "Didn't I tell you earlier?"

At the first light of morning, when they let the goats out, the walaga jumped up and leaped away into the bush. His accelerating hooves beat out the story: "Fara n saon–fara n saon–fara n saon–fara n saon . . . etc.!" ("Fara n saon" means "the bush is better, the bush is better, the bush is better.")

"The grass is greener..." is probably a universal false perception. The human organism tends to always believe that his present circumstances are unfavorable. The African catechist might very well use a story as above to illustrate the significance of what the apostle Paul had to say in Philippians 4:

I have learned to be content whatever the circumstances. I know what it is to be in need, and I know what it is to have plenty. I have learned the secret of being content in any and every situation, whether well fed or hungry, whether living in plenty or in want. I can do everything through him who gives me strength (Philippians 4:11-13).

Some of us learn the lesson of how well-off we really are only after a narrow brush with disaster, as the walaga experienced. Some of us, in our state of dissatisfaction, jump too quickly into a greener pasture and feel the knife of cir-

## 29.  Fleeing Antelope.

cumstances for a wrong decision. May this humorous African story help us to be good "counters of the cost" before we leap.

### Note

1. Paul G. Bretscher, *The World Upside-Down or Rightside-Up?* (St. Louis: Concordia Publishing House, 1964).

# Conclusion

The communication charts or models that are used to illustrate the components of the theory of communication are useful in the west. These models always contain a component called *context*. This book has been a study of the contextualization of African theological concepts basically aimed at the western mind set.

## The Role of Context in Perception

You have perhaps seen this little jingle before somewhere:
GODISNOWHERE.
Scanning from left to right, as we are taught to do in the west, the reader searches the grouping of letters to break them down from an unrecognizable cluster into something "meaningful." The reader can quickly separate it into two short sentences. You can "see" either: GOD IS NOW HERE or GOD IS NO WHERE. The author does not mean to insult the reader's intelligence, but only to suggest that if one hundred people were given this twelve letter "word" and asked what they see, there is a good chance that those with a predisposition about the existence of God (or not) would

be influenced by that mental perception. Many people, of course, would see both possibilities.

The function of context in perception is similar to this. The mind seems to recognize what it already knows much quicker and with less energy than when required to figure out something new, or to perceive an alternate form from that which is comfortable or habitual.

My task has been to break through the expectations of the reader's perceptual world, trying to move the participant into a world of another people and time frame. One of the large goals of the writer was to bring the reader to ask the question: "What part of the way I interpret the Bible, or have been taught to perceive the scripture, has been influenced by my culture and cognitive perceptual field?" Of course, some may read these pages from a sociological context where the issue of biblical interpretation was secondary.

## Parables and Truth

It is well documented that West African cultures value the power of parable to teach or illustrate truth. Africans have believed for centuries, and still believe today, that one of the best ways to inculcate values and ideas in the minds of their young is to create a parabolic problem and ask them to solve it. This is not done individually but collectively as children and young people of a certain "age group" learn the tribal expectations of adulthood together. Learning together—this is such a good description of what happens in traditional West African society.

An astonishing percentage of western educated young people grow up to strongly dislike the whole educational process. This is generally untrue of West African youth. Why the difference? Thirty years of experience leads me to conclude that oral/aural societies which give a predisposition to narrative as a teaching method somehow condition youth with a desire to learn. This curiosity and love of learning remains all of their lives. From ages 3 to 93, West Africans love the learning process. Does communal teaching through narrative and parable help create the difference in basic attitudes about learning that would account for the difference? This is a question that needs further research which might have pedagogical importance.

The study of the book of Revelation in the New Testament could probably profit from employing the circular Hebrew world view of *time* in place of the West's linear/sequential temporal mode. Just so, these chapters have tried to illustrate that traditional West African society, being culturally closer to the original matrix from which the scriptures have come to us, often have a hermeneutical advantage for biblical interpretation. African-American readers should take pride in the demonstration, by these chapters, that deep treasures of ancient knowledge, about which they were given little information, can help explain the most widely read book in existence! Communicologists should find examples here for illustrating the need for intercultural perception.

The author would be content to be perceived as being a little entertaining while enlarging, even in the smallest of measures, the unlimited scope of understanding of the Book of Books! I am forever grateful to Africa's noble people.

# Glossary of African Words

ADZE LE GBE NAM: A Ewe phrase of fear that any sudden voice "hitch" or hoarseness might be related to witchcraft or a curse.

ASHANTI: A strong and resistant tribe in central Ghana with a colorful and powerful social system of dual rulers both matrilineal and patrilineal.

BIDEM, BIDEM: The onomatopoetic sound of someone handicapped trying to run.

BUDA, BUDA... The sound (onomatopoeia) the Mossi would use to describe a person walking in loose fitting sandals.

BUDU: Mori word designating a person who is either a kinsman or someone so liked as to be considered a kinsman.

CALABASH: A circular gourd of up to 18 inches in diameter used in West African drum making.

CATECHIST: A French word used in Africa to designate someone who teaches religion as a vocation (a preacher not necessarily ordained to ministry.)

EWE: A major West African tribe living in Togo and Ghana (2,300,000). Language: Ewe

FARA N SAON-FARA N SAON: Another Mossi word use of the meaning and sound of pronunciation that coincide (onomatopoeia) "The bush is better—the bush is better."

FURDURDURDA: Onomatopoetic sound of liquid running. The Mossi love onomatopoeia.

GA SOABA: Mossi word describing a valued and trusted friend.

GRIOT: A French word used to describe an African ceremonial "singer" who recounts the past in song at official tribal functions of community importance.

GUINEA HEN: The female of guinea fowl. A fowl the size of a chicken, gray in color, growing in the wild and indigenous to Africa. As domesticated, they are desirable but less valuable than chickens.

IGBO: Tribe of many millions living in eastern Nigeria. The Igbo sought independence during the Biafran civil war in the late 1960s.

KASENA: Tribe in southern Burkina-Faso and northern Ghana whose language is Kasem. In contrast to the Mossi, they do not have a strong central chief social structure.

KEM YUURE: A Mori term meaning literally "elder's name." The chief's "nom de guerre" is never spoken. Traditionally, a wife never speaks her husband's name. "Kem yuure" is a substitute just as the Jews don't say or write the name of God but substitute another word in its place.

KIIMA: A Mossi term for a particular spirit or apparition.

KOURS, KOURS/KO,KO,KO: An African tale properly told always includes significant sounds. These are the sounds of the hoe's head while digging, and the hoe's handle knocking on a tree branch.

KUIS: A Mori word describing all the activity surrounding the actual physical "delivery" of a new wife from and by her family members into the household of the father of her future children.

LUNGA: A drum with two heads of goat's skin. Pitch becomes highly variable by modifying internal pressure through constriction and release of leather thongs connecting the heads. Figuratively, a person called a "lunga" is two-faced and unstable. "He speaks out of both sides of his mouth."

MANE SUGRI: A Mori phrase translated "make a covering." "Make a covering for me" is a request for forgiveness.

MORO NABA: The Mori word for emperor. He was the highest power in the land. There has been a Mossi emperor since the 13th century.

MOSSI: Dominant tribe living in Burkina-Faso (6,000,000). Language: Mori.

NABIIGA: Literally: "I noticed that you recognized me."

NABASSEGA: The most important yearly festival for the Mossi. It is the annual renewal of the forces of nature that insures fertility of crops and women, plus prosperity and health.

NABUGA: The heir apparent son (or nephew) of the Moro Naba. His education by the tribal elders was unique and extensive.

NE TUMDE: Literally: "I am honoring your personhood by recognizing that you are working."

NOMMO: A Bantu word for spirit/supernatural power obtained with secret words.

NOOGO: Mori word for sweet.

OLUNGAWEMA: The name of a mythical fruit tree.

PUSH-LIPP PUUSH-LIPP: The onomatopoetic name for the walk of a lion.

SAGALEM, SAGALEM: The onomatopoetic name for the walk of an elephant.

SAHEL: Narrow band of semi-arid land stretching east to west over 4,000 miles from Senegal to Ethiopia between the Sahara on the north and well watered land to the south.

SOUNOOGO: Mori word for happiness (literally: heart sweetness)

SOURI: Mori word for heart.

SOUSAONGO: Mori word for sadness (literally: spoiled heart)

TENKOUKA: A Mori word for the kapok tree standing prominently in the village. Animists may attribute special power to the tree and sacrifice animals at its roots seeking some favor.

TUULLE: A Mossi term for a particular spirit or apparition.

WALAGA: Small antelope weighing about 25-30 pounds, which the Mossi love to eat.

YAREDO NE TAABA: A Mori concept that means a covenant bond between two people that totally transcends objects and ownership. Deep affection between non-kin individuals who choose to make such a covenant.

YELL-PAKRE-TIM: A superstitious belief in supernatural intervention and protection in face of life-threatening circumstances.

ZOUGOU: Mori word for head.

ZOUNOOGO: Mori word for luck.

# General Index

# Scripture Index